T5-BAF-329

DISCARDED
FROM
UNIVERSITY OF DAYTON
ROESCH LIBRARY

THE MARIANISTS
10 Sawmill Road
Dayton, Ohio 45409

# ON BEING YOURSELF

Reflections
on
Spirituality and Originality

ADRIAN VAN KAAM, C.S.Sp.

DIMENSION BOOKS, INC.
Denville, New Jersey

*Published by Dimension Books*
*Denville, New Jersey*

**Imprimi Potest:**  *Rev. Charles P. Connors, C. S. Sp.*
*Provincial*

**Nihil Obstat:**  *Rev. William J. Winter, S. T. D.*
*Censor Librorum*

**Imprimatur:**  *Most Rev. Vincent M. Leonard, D. D.*
*Bishop of Pittsburgh*

*July 7, 1972*

BX
23
6

Grateful acknowledgement is hereby made to Alfred A. Knopf, Inc. for excerpts from *Markings* by Dag Hammarskjold, Translation Copyright ©1964 by Alfred A. Knopf, Inc.

Copyright 1972 by Adrian van Kaam

All rights reserved. No part of this book may be reproduced in any form without written permission from the publisher, except for brief passages included in a review appearing in a newspaper or magazine.

MARIAN

53766

# CONTENTS

# PREFACE

This book of reflections on originality in the light of spirituality could be read as a complement to my book *ENVY AND ORIGINALITY* (Doubleday & Co., 1972) in which originality is studied in the light of the human sciences. The latter book is a more systematic one while the following reflections are less strictly structured as a whole. Each reflection forms a unity in itself and can be read on its own. Yet the theme of spirituality and originality binds all these reflections together and is developed in such a way that only a reading of all the reflections will do justice to the topic. While it is not necessary to read *ENVY AND ORIGINALITY*, it may be enlightening for the interested reader to turn to this book before or after his reading of these reflections. Such reading may clarify the dynamics of original growth and its obstacles, both of which are presupposed in this book.

It is my pleasant obligation to express my gratefulness to my colleagues Father E. J. van Croonenburg, C.S.Sp., D.Th., and Dr. S.A. Muto, Ph.D., for their careful reading of the manuscript and their suggestions for improvement in style and content.

# I
## ORIGINALITY AND
## CHRISTIAN SPIRITUALITY

Dag Hammar-
skjöld was a remarkable man—not only because of his
contribution to the United Nations as Secretary-
General but more so for his spiritual life. His diary,
*Markings,* was discovered after his death. It brought
to light his inward journey. Hammarskjöld's spirituality is different from that of the Far East. Eastern
mysticism aims at man's fusion with the Sacred, his
disappearance in the totality of all that is. Christian
spirituality stresses the opposite.

The Christian believes that he originates from God
as a unique person. The Eternal Father calls him in
Christ to be himself out of love for God and man. To
be sure, Christian spirituality speaks about giving up
myself, forgetting myself, dying to the old man. This
does not mean, however, that a Christian should lose
his identity or fuse with the Godhead. It means that
as a Christian, I should distance myself from false
self-images. I should not strive after an isolated God-
like self. I must give up self-centered plans and

projects. I must find my original self as hidden in God. The original life of a Christian, as St. Paul says, is hidden in Christ. The Eternal Father originates each one of us in Him.

Each person is called to become his own self and yet to become at-one with God. I must become the unique person I am meant to be. The more I become what my Creator called me to be originally, the more I will be united with my Divine Origin. This union with my Origin deepens my originality. Mine is an originality that God wills from eternity. He originated me as precisely this person and nobody else.

Hammarskjöld's diary reveals one man's search for his original mission, which is at the same time the search of every man. At the end of his life, this search seems to have been crowned by God's intervention. Man cannot look so deeply into his own unique calling without a special enlightenment of God—a light that burns and illumines at the same time. In the end, Hammarskjöld seems to have received this light. The beginning of his diary talks about his human search for what he is originally called to be. Only the last part of his journal seems to indicate that a divine force began to permeate his human effort.

The initial search for his original self is expressed in the following:

> At every moment you choose yourself. But do you choose *your* self? Body and soul contain a thousand possibilities out of which you can build many *I's*. But in only one of them is there a congruence of the elector and the elected. Only one—which you will never find

until you have excluded all those superficial and fleeting possibilities of being and doing with which you toy, out of curiosity or wonder or greed, and which hinder you from casting anchor in the experience of the mystery of life, and the consciousness of the talent entrusted to you which is your *I.* (p. 19. Dag Hammarskjöld. *Markings.* New York: Alfred A. Knopf, 1969. All subsequent quotations are from this edition and are indicated by page number.)

To be truly human means to choose your true self. Everything you decide makes you be in a certain way. It builds your life in a certain direction. This is true of your decision regarding *what* to do. It is also true of your decision regarding *how* to do it. Your life situation may have imposed on you already what you should do. One thing remains up to you always and that is *how* to *uniquely* do what you are doing.

How do you put your self in your daily tasks, in your contacts with people, the care of your family, or the playing of sports? You can do these things in a thousand ways, but only one way can build the original you that God called you to be.

There are many tempting possibilities of being yourself in a false way. They are at odds with God's plan for your life. You try to be somebody you are not called to be. You do so to please others. You crave to be liked. You hanker after success, applause, possession. These ways cannot be truly yours. They hinder you from casting anchor in the life of Christ hidden deep within you. It is only in Him that you find yourself as God is calling you.

Hammarskjöld courageously tried to recognize his hidden self-centered ambitions. He exposed the public person he was tempted to substitute for his real self. He writes:

He seeks his own comfort—
and is rewarded with glimpses of satisfaction followed
    by a long period of emptiness and shame which
    sucks him dry.
He fights for his position—
all his talk about the necessary preconditions for doing
    something worthwhile prove an insecure barrier
    against self-disgust.
He devotes himself to his job—
but he is in doubt as to its importance and therefore,
    constantly looking for recognition . . . (p. 36)

Hammarskjöld feels the pain we all feel when others condemn us. They may ridicule us when we go the way of our original self in Christ. They chide us for not walking the public path. Being yourself often makes you unacceptable to this world. Following your unique calling in Christ implies accepting the condemnation of the world. It is part of the journey from a merely public life to an original life before God. As Hammarskjöld says to himself:

You asked for burdens to carry—And howled when they
were placed on your shoulders . . .
O Caesarea Philippi: to accept condemnation on the
Way as its fulfillment, its definition, to accept
this both when it is chosen and when it is realized.
    (p. 36)

Hammarskjöld comes to know his original self. He begins to discover Christ as his example. He meditates upon Jesus approaching His end: "A young man, adamant in his committed life . . . an adamant young man, alone as he confronted his final destiny . . . ." This quotation brings to light our likeness with Christ and helps us to be adamant like He was, to stand alone when confronted with our original calling.

Hammarskjöld, then, learned to see his original commitment in light of the life of Jesus:

How proper it is that Christmas should follow Advent. — For him who looks towards the future, the Manger is situated on Golgotha, and the Cross has already been raised in Bethlehem. (p. 198)

The last mention of Jesus is in his Whitsunday 1961 meditation in *Markings:*

As I continued along the Way, I learned, step by step, word by word, that behind every saying in the Gospels stands *one* man and *one* man's experience. Also behind the prayer that the cup might pass from him and his promise to drink it. Also behind each of the words from the Cross. (p. 205)

Hammarskjöld becomes aware that his originality is hidden in God. To be oneself is to suffer loneliness. Our Lord suffered loneliness in His original calling. Hammarskjöld is consoled knowing that this Lord is in him. He is called to share the burden of the Lord. He must be faithful to his own originality as Jesus was to His—faithful unto death like Christ Himself.

Thou who has created us free, Who seest all that happens
   —yet are confident of victory,
   Thou who at this time art the one among us who
   suffereth the uttermost loneliness,

## ON BEING YOURSELF

> Thou—who are also in me,
> May I bear Thy burden, when my hour comes,
> May I- (p. 98)

Finally his human asceticism becomes a Christian asceticism surrendered to God, dependent on God, no longer counting on human strength. This turn is movingly expressed in Hammarskjöld's humble prayer:

> Have mercy
> Upon us.
> Have mercy
> Upon our efforts,
> That we
> Before Thee,
> In love and in faith,
> Righteousness and humility,
> May follow Thee,
> With self-denial, steadfastness and courage,
> And meet Thee
> in the silence.
>
> Give us
> A pure heart
> That we may see Thee,
> A humble heart
> That we may hear Thee,
> A heart of love
> That we may serve Thee,
> A heart of faith
> That we may live Thee.
>
> Thou
> Whom I do not know
> But Whose I am.

> Thou
> Whom I do not comprehend
> But Who hast dedicated me
> To my fate.
> Thou — (pp. 214-215)

## *Spiritual Search and Search for Self*

Hammarskjöld's spiritual search was tied to a search for himself. His life shows what the lives of other men have shown before: that the spiritual life of one person cannot be a carbon copy of that of another. I have to find the meaning of my spiritual life and live this life in my own way.

I may feel that the meaning of my life is already laid down once and for all in writings, rules, and examples. It seems as if all I have to do is take this wisdom in and file it away. The more I file away, the better will be my possibilities for spiritual growth. The meanings I take in differ in no way from those you take in provided you read the same books, follow the same traditions, go through the same spiritual exercises, and reflect upon the same examples as I.

In this way I would become spiritual, alike in life, thought, mood, and feeling with others who have followed the same procedure. In that case, however, my spiritual life would not really be my own. There would be nothing distinctive about it.

Initiation into the spiritual life would mean merely a gathering of pertinent information, practicing the proper exercises, reading the most relevant books. Spirituality would not bring out my uniqueness as a person, called to manifest the presence of the Divine in a special and unrepeatable way.

### Personal and Shared Spiritual Meaning

Such a programmed approach would not work. Why not? The answer is simple. Because I am not the same as others. My body is different. So is my mind, my temperament, my mood, my personal history, my predisposition for vices and virtues.

The idea that my spiritual life is already laid down for me by others points to a partial truth. In some sense I find the meaning of my life outside myself. It remains equally true, however, that I find the meaning of my life within me.

No man is an island. I am always with others. If I am not with them bodily, I am still touched by their influence that lingers on in my life, even in solitude.

Were I to visit China, all Chinese might at first look alike to me. They wear the same clothes, do the same things, stick to the same customs, use the same expressions. Only later on do I realize that each Chinese shows traits of his own, that each carries on the Chinese tradition in his way. He is not merely a Chinese like an orange tree is an orange tree. He is a human person who assimilates the customs of his culture personally. He remains nevertheless a true Chinese, for he casts his life in the universally recognizable forms of a distinctive Chinese culture.

The same is true for me. I can live a Christian life

because I have grown up in traditions of Christian spirituality, which I find already alive in my religion and culture. This Christian spiritual life becomes uniquely mine as I begin to draw the universal meanings of these traditions into my own history of personal experience.

I am born into a world already rich in spiritual significance. Parents, brothers, sisters, and fellow men live in a world full of personal and spiritual meaning. Into this world I am inserted. I drink in its meanings eagerly, but the way in which I take them in is shaped by my originality. This world of meaning becomes truly mine.

As a Christian, I am inserted into a Christian universe of meaning. At the center of this universe are the sacred words of the New Testament. The spiritual life of each believer draws on these words. Christian spirituality stands or falls by its fidelity to the Lord's Revelation. His words carry the same meaning for all of us. That makes us alike as Christians. Yet the same words can also drive home a message different for each person or even different for the same person at different times of his life.

Let me give an example. Any text will do. Take the words of the *Book of Revelation:* "Here I stand, knocking at the door. If anyone hears me calling and opens the door, I will enter his house and have supper with him and he with me" (Rev. 3:20).

These words carry the same basic meaning for all Christians. The Lord invites all men to the messianic banquet in heaven. Beyond this common meaning, I may feel that this text carries a special meaning for me. This meaning may vary with my personality and with the particular phase I am in at this moment of my life.

The Lord's knocking at the door may mean He is asking me to give up an attachment which makes it difficult for me to open up to the life of prayer or I may sense that He is inviting me to be more kind to a suffering person for whom I feel little compassion. I may feel that Christ is knocking at the door of my life, that the Lord implores me to use my talents to improve the world in which I am living. On the other hand, I may see that the Lord asks me to give up some of my involvements in social enterprises. Perhaps He is calling me to become more contemplative. Or I may experience that this message means that I should give myself to my fellow men by allowing my Lord, in and through me, to foster social justice.

Many more "enlightenments" may flow from these words in the *Book of Revelation*. The potential personal meanings of a holy text are inexhaustible. What a text under God's Grace means to me depends on the numerous influences that shape my world of meaning. These influences may be cultural, historical, educational, familial. Permeating all of them is the influence we would call personal or original.

*Personal Appropriation of Meaning*

I am called to make my own the insights of Chris-

tian spirituality. I find these meanings first of all in
the life and words of Jesus, further in sermons, talks,
rules, exercises, examples, and spiritual writings.
When I assimilate these truths of Christian experience, I may become their origin in my own spiritual
world of meaning. This does not necessarily imply that
my meanings are different from those of others. What
it means is that I have made them so much my own
that I am at home with them.

My at-homeness with spiritual truths does not
necessarily reveal itself in the content of my experiences which may be the same for me as for other
people. What is personal is the way in which I take in
and bring out these same experiences. Let us go back
to our example, the words of the *Book of Revelation:*
"Here I stand, knocking at the door." We saw the
way in which these words can be taken personally.
Once these words have touched me, once I have dwelt
upon them in my own way, when I talk about them,
others will hear a note of personal experience. It
strikes them immediately. My words carry a message.

A deeply spiritual man like the saintly pastor of
Ars drew people from all over. He did not strike them
as a mighty preacher like Bossuet or a brilliant mind
like Pascal. The pastor of Ars had been a poor student
in the seminary, a problem case for his professors.
What he talked about in his pulpit was not new. It
was the simple message of the Gospel. He told it
often in tired clichés and worn out metaphors. But
burning in and behind the old words was the intense

experience of this small emaciated man. That is what turned the people on, so to speak.

I am not a saint like the pastor of Ars. Yet what I have taken in personally will be brought out in a more compelling way than what has not yet become my own. People may say of me: "He is so convincing," or "He is so with it." For people can feel a difference between two expressions of the same insight. One expression may be simply the communication of what I have heard or read somewhere. Another expression reveals me as a person who has dwelt upon what he has heard or read. The same content may be communicated, but the second mode of communication says something deeper. In addition to information, I impart an original experience. I invite my listener to make this experience his own.

Spirituality is not only a matter of information. It should foster in the person an assimilation of these insights. I must become the origin of my spiritual world of meaning, not just a specialist who has filed away so much information. In the light of Grace, I must make my own the insights granted to me.

*Be Original*

We can bring together in two words all we have said thus far. Be original! To be original means that I am the origin of what I think, feel, say, and do. To be original does not mean, however, that I am the origin of my inner and outer acts in an ultimate and independent way.

Let us illustrate this idea with an example from nature. Lake Victoria is the origin of the Nile, but it is not its independent origin. For the existence and power of Lake Victoria itself depends on other factors. Lake Victoria has received its water from other sources, from the earth and from the sky; it obtained its monumental shape and majestic power not by itself alone but in and through many chance events during long periods of geological history. Now the Lake exists in its own form. It has its own personality, as it were. And as such, it is the origin of the mighty Nile.

The same is true for me. I cannot be an independent origin of my spiritual life. I have to draw constantly on the Grace of God. As we have seen, spiritual life is always tied to the spiritual traditions and meanings which I find in my religion and culture. I wear the cloak of Christian spirituality but I wear it in my own size. Moreover, Christian spirituality turns out a variety of cloaks. Think only of the difference between the spiritualities of Francis of Assisi and Ignatius of Loyola, Teresa of Avila and Thérèse of Lisieux, John Bosco and Francis Libermann. I may choose a cloak which suits my taste and even then I should fit it to my size.

The longer I wear a suit, dress, or pair of shoes, the more they take on the shape of my body, torso, and feet. A new suit feels strange and uneasy. After wearing it for some time, it becomes more mine. It loses its former stiffness. It takes on something of my personality, and yet it is the same suit I once bought to show off proudly at the office party for the boss.

The same is true of the form of spiritual life I choose. It too becomes gradually mine. My original personality begins to shine through it. No longer is it what it was at first. Yet nobody looks surprised. My life strikes other people as familiar. Their attitude shows that to be original is not necessarily to be peculiar or different.

I may be of the belief that originality means to attract undue attention. There is after all a kind of originality that is conspicuous. Some people do more than make their own customs, traditions, and meanings they inherit. They break old ways down. They push new ideas forward. They stand out as different not only from their neighbors but also from the established culture as a whole.

Yet, even such inventive people do not create in a vacuum. They may go beyond the generally accepted cultural views and values. Still they are in touch with other more hidden trends in the culture. They cut through the established culture to unearth subterranean currents. They bring latent tendencies into the open. They give form and name to what was formerly nameless.

I must make my own the spiritual meanings of my culture and religion if I want them to come to life in me. The same is true for the rare person who gives form to vague and hidden aspirations in the culture. He must make these aspirations his own while giving form to them. Were he simply satisfied with giving form to scattered ideas alive in the underground of society, without making these his own, then he himself would not foster his personal growth as a spiritual man.

It is important to keep in mind the distinction between an inventive kind of originality—what we could call a "cultural originality"—and the personal originality about which we have spoken. Otherwise I may confuse the one with the other. I may begin to feel that I can only live a spiritual life if I do things out of the ordinary. When I cannot pull off such feats, I may be tempted to throw the towel in altogether. Let us, therefore, look more closely at the difference between cultural and personal originality.

## Cultural Originality

I may be the origin of such new cultural forms as words, rites, theories, systems, or symbols which publicly express and foster spirituality in my culture. For instance, I may introduce a new style of religious poetry. I may inspire renewal in patterns of worship. I may create a new theology or start a social movement that embodies the religious concerns of my fellow men. I act as a catalyst of hidden needs already stirring people and groping for expression.

As a culturally original person, I am endowed with a fine radar for such trends. Cultural originality does not guarantee the growth of the innovator. I may not live spiritually at all and still be alive as a maker of new theologies. I may be dead as a spiritual man and alive as a socio-religious agitator. I myself may not profit spiritually from my own cultural insights, while my fellow men may draw inspiration from them.

I am called to live an original spiritual life in the personal sense. Yet I may not be original culturally. This is nothing to be sad about. I may be less distracted by public acclaim and demands, less tempted to a pride that closes me off from the mystery of Grace.

Nevertheless, public regard for religious inventiveness, especially in times of change, may tempt me to pretend that I too am an inventive person. I may try to look unusual in the public eye. I may strive after a conspicuous originality in the realm of religion. Such make-believe creativity leads to hollow religious expressions. It deforms me as a person.

I can be original without being outwardly different, I can be outwardly different without being inwardly original.

*Personal Originality*

Personal originality implies that I live in my own way the customs and traditions of spirituality that are already available in my culture. I may not feel called to initiate a new form of prayer, another theology, or a religious movement. I may live the same spiritual knowledge, expressions, and customs as others do. What is original is the personal way in which I live them. I make these expressions of spirituality my own.

Rather than accept them for their own sake, I see them as occasions to discover and live my own spiritual life.

The structures of spirituality I share with other men are many and varied. They form a treasure trove of possibilities. In and through them I can embody, express and nourish my own life of prayer.

Take, for example, the meditative reading of the Gospel. The first Christians listened thoughtfully to the oral traditions about the life of Jesus. They dwelt on His life personally. Each one asked himself, "What does Jesus mean for me at this moment of my life?" They tried to discover a personal relevance in the good news they heard. The oral tradition that proved most stimulating for Christian spirituality was written into the books of the New Testament. From then on, Christians in family and religious community engaged in the meditative reading of these books together or alone.

This custom of spiritual reading can be adopted in a formal way. I can read the Gospel faithfully for fifteen minutes a day. I can do it as a duty hastily going through the pages to fill up the time. It can be said that I punctually engage in one of the traditional customs of Christian spirituality. The fact is, however, that I am satisfied with this informational and merely dutiful reading of the Gospel. I do not attempt to make its message personal. I do not listen to the Holy Spirit in me. My reading may thus deplete my spiritual life instead of nourishing it.

## From Mere Custom to Lived Experience

I must render Christian customs of spirituality original by trying to animate them with my openness to the Holy Spirit. He must find me ready when He deigns to communicate His light to me. Then these customs may be transformed to living experiences. An expression of spirituality mechanically performed is despiritualizing.

Traditions of spirituality will remain dead for me if I do not animate them with my originality. It is my challenge to fill these expressions with personal meaning, to rejoice in their resurrection. I should not expect dead customs to come to life overnight. It is even possible that some traditions cannot be revitalized at all, for they are too far removed from present day reality.

Christian spirituality is first of all nourished by the Eucharistic celebration and the sacraments. The personalized reading of the Bible, however, the original saying of the Holy Office, the prayers before and after meals, are not separated from this sacramental life. These practices are nourished by reception of the sacraments. These personalized exercises in turn prepare for this sacramental life and keep it alive. The customs and traditions of spirituality are meant to ready me for the gifts that come to me in and through the sacramental life of the Church, but they can only do so if I make them truly my own.

# II
## PRESENCE TO MY ORIGIN

I find in my deepest self the mystery of my own Origin, which is the Origin of all that is. In these depths I feel at-one with God. I feel also at-one with every person and thing that emerges from this same Divine Ground. On the deepest level of my life, it is no longer possible to distinguish a vertical relationship to God and a horizontal relationship to man. I can no longer see the one without at least implicitly experiencing the other.

Spirituality could be described as the attempt to integrate myself in light of this presence to my Origin. The last part of this sentence is crucial. As spirit, I am openness to my Origin. I may not realize this explicitly. My technical civilization may have obscured the awareness that every man *is* spiritual. As spirit, man is already openness to something that transcends his emotional and practical involvements as an organizing self.

Spirituality implies certain structures, dynamics, and laws of development. These are basically the same for all men no matter to what culture or religion they belong. There is a fundamental human spirituality. This basic spirituality becomes specified in accordance with the culture or religion in which a person lives.

The Sacred has revealed Itself to me as Holy Trinity and has incarnated Itself in Christ. To the natural wisdom of spirituality a revealed truth has been added. It gives me a certitude infinitely greater than anything I could derive from my natural knowledge. Revelation sheds new light on the natural life of the spirit. It helps me to distinguish more clearly between what is essential and what is accidental. As Thomas Aquinas asserted, grace and revelation do not make superfluous natural structures and dynamics of the spirit; they enhance and deepen what has been given to man as his most beautiful potential: the gift to live spiritually.

## Integrating Power of This Presence

My awareness is spread out over many things. I am preoccupied with my responsibilities. I am involved in ambitions, cares, and concerns, many of which may be necessary for my survival, growth, and effectiveness. I have to develop and maintain a culture. I must fulfill my duty toward family, nation, and the wider human community. These many involvements can make me restless and tense, rob me of peace, joy, and resiliency.

Within the dispersion of daily endeavors, I must discover a meaning which integrates my experience.

*Presence to My Origin*

This meaning can be found in presence to something that goes beyond particular involvements and at the same time permeates and sustains them. The more I live in light of this Presence, the more I will be able to experience my works, dreams, tensions, and worries as patterns of a meaningful whole. I must allow my origin in the Sacred to dominate my life as the ultimate meaning of all I am and do. I may then regain the lost wholeness I seek.

The example and sustaining force of my self-integration is Christ Himself. The meaning of His life is found in His Presence to the Will of the Father as the Divine Origin of all that is and occurs. Living in obedience to the Divine Will made Christ's life a unity. He promised His peace to those who would live in the light of His example. He called His a peace the world cannot give. "I tell you all this that in me you may find peace. You will suffer in the world. But take courage! I have overcome the world " (John 16:33). His peace goes far deeper than the contentment derived from worldly goods. It is the fruit of a spiritual life, nourished by grace. His is a peace found also in suffering, misunderstanding, and failure, a peace that passes understanding.

*Presence to My Origin and Presence to Others*

Presence to my Origin helps me to meet in love and respect any person or thing that may appear in my life situation. Without this experience, it may demand strenuous effort on my part to respect certain people. They may be vicious, envious, fanatically conservative, or fanatically progressive. I may have to engage in long-winded reasonings to convince myself that I should love them. I may attempt to appreciate them merely on basis of a logical conclusion deduced from the premise that, after all, they too are created by God and redeemed by Christ. I may succeed in the right behavior by such repeated religious reasonings about how to manage human relationships, but my comportment with such people can only become spontaneous when it flows from the experience of the other as sharing with me God's creating and maintaining Presence.

In the solitude of the spirit, I find neighbor and nature as intimately united with me. I feel at-one with them in our coming forth from a shared and Sacred Origin, in our being called together to redemption and salvation. Prayerful presence to my Origin is the condition for charity. It enables me to respect everyone and everything as they appear on the horizon of my daily life.

When people see themselves and each other in the light of their Divine Origin, they are born again. They see themselves and each other anew. They recognize how each one comes forth from God uniquely. They realize how one Origin speaks in all originalities. They feel at-one in this vision. The experience of each one's uniqueness could have divided them. It would have done so if they were not illuminated by the mystery of Divine Presence that encompasses us all.

Religious awareness of my uniqueness is at the same time an experience of at-oneness, a divine at-oneness that surpasses our differences. This awareness can become so deep in a saintly person that it will not be destroyed by disappointment, anger, and conflict. These feelings may ripple the surface of his personality but will not disrupt its core.

## *Presence to My Origin and Presence to the Struggle of Life*

Presence to the mysterious Divine Origin of my life does not mean that I escape the struggle, effort, and conflict of humanity on its way to a better world. It makes me share more courageously in this struggle. To dwell inwardly in my Divine Origin is a source of personal strength, often disposing me to concrete acts of courage. The spiritual man is not a fugitive from the fight for social justice. *If* God calls him to be in the midst of this fight, the deep calm of his spiritual life carries him like a ship carries its fighting soldiers.

An aircraft carrier viewed from above strikes us as a calm vessel; its awesome deck sustains equipment and manpower for battle. The ship is tossed by the sea. Unperturbed, it plows its way through the waves. Its majestic calm makes efficient battle possible. Similarly, immersed in the calm of my Origin, I will be better able to engage in the battle of mankind for a better world *if* this would be my mission. Pressure, struggle, and action will test the truth and the strength of my presence to God. If I cannot stand up under duress, it may be because my presence to God is no more than a soothing experience, a form of self-indulgence, an idle fantasy to while away the time.

If I live in true presence, however, I participate in a world far more original than that of concrete daily events; I live also in the hidden world at the root of all happenings. I am not so overwhelmed then by distress.

Awareness of my Sacred Origin has the power to uplift me to a serenity which no conflict or suffering can disturb. Yet to live in this awareness does not imply selfish placidity; it does not remove me from the anguish and effort of the common life. On the contrary, I am better equipped to stand up under the pressures and conflicts of daily existence. I feel stronger and wiser because I realize that our Eternal Origin originates each one of us uniquely.

This awareness renews vitality and dignity. I feel called to be a unique presence in this world. Feeling rooted in something that surpasses all events, I am no longer wholly at the mercy of these changing times. Return to my Origin enables me to discern the real from the illusory. It liberates my judgment. My outlook is no longer limited by the immediate appearances of people, events, and things. I become peacefully aware that a Divine Origin allows them to be in their own way. The same Divine Origin lets me be in my own way and asks me to make the best of all that happens. This vision confers a calm and certitude which no disaster can wreck.

In that divine composure, new aspects of my situation are disclosed to me. I arrive at new judgments and actions, which usually turn out to be more realistic and effective. I am no longer overwhelmed by the happenings around me. I can see beyond them. I can locate them against a wider horizon.

"Where there is no vision, the people perish." The same can be said of each one of us. I can lose the awareness of my original calling. In this case, my vision may not go beyond the interests and enthusiasms of the public and the public media. I am controlled instead of being in control. Swept along by the mass of men, I no longer know who I truly am. I become a social robot. I am defeated as a person, and all because I have lost the vision of my originality as rooted in the Divine Will.

I can be myself only when I keep my spiritual life active and vigorous. The spiritual life is as much a part of man's life as every other dimension. Until I realize this life in me, I am not fully a man; my chances of being faithful to my originality are consequently slim.

To find myself in this deeper spiritual sense will not diminish but enhance my original gifts and life style. The spiritual life will increase my wisdom and steadfastness. It will help me to respect better than ever before the original calling of each man. The spiritual life will help me to see my daily life and surroundings in truer perspective, discerning the Eternal Origin beyond and beneath apparent fragmentation. Spiritual life will instill in me a respectful love unmarred by sentimentalism or selfishness. Presence to my Origin will fill me with quiet assurance in hours of crisis and defeat.

Spiritual life could be thus described as a unique union of my original being with the all-pervading Origin of myself and of all that is.

## Presence to My Origin and the Managing Me

I can face myself and my environment from different viewpoints. Driving through heavy traffic, the only thing I am preoccupied with is my driving. Everything I see or do is drawn into this actual concern here and now. I look at the people who cross the road before my car; I do not see them as persons with interesting faces but as hazards to be avoided. I may cast a hasty eye on trees and utility poles, walls of houses, fences of gardens as I pass them by. At this moment they do not strike me as beautiful or ugly, cold or cozy. They serve as guideposts. They lay out for me the limits of the road on which I have to stay. My brakes and gas pedal do not stand out as gadgets for me to try out playfully. They have turned into practical tools; by means of them I must time my speed carefully. I do not hold my eyes on the rear view mirror to catch the reflection of my face or the fascinating scenes that unfold behind me. I have set my mirror so that I can bring into my field of vision anything that may endanger my car when passed by or passing another car.

Briefly, I must stick to those aspects of my environment that have a practical meaning for my driving. I am only interested now in managing my situation during rush hour traffic in such a way that I safely reach home. When I shift into this practical organizing outlook on reality, my self becomes a "managing me." Without this practical concentration on my car, the road and the traffic, I may not end up at home but in a hospital or cemetery.

My managing self is at work in all my daily practical undertakings—study, cooking, sports, socializing. I have to get in touch with the immediate practical sides of concepts, people, and things when I want to do something concrete in the world. Even my highest ideals cannot be realized if I do not use my ability to manage reality.

Let us say I resolve to spend some time daily in meditation. To make this promise come true, I must pick a good time and place; I must drop certain activities or assign them to other moments, perhaps skip some T.V., and plan carefully how to slip away from family and friends for such occasions. It takes practical planning to ready myself for daily meditation. Without my managing self, I could not inscribe my intentions and my ideals in the world. My managing me is the instrument of daily incarnation, the bridge between my spirit and everyday reality.

Once I meditate, however, the scene shifts. My practical outlook relaxes; the manager in me becomes silent. No longer am I glued to the immediate practical aspects of my environment. I try to look at the deeper meanings of life. My outlook at this moment is not that of the managing me but of the spirit. The spiritual dimension of myself comes to the fore; the managing dimension recedes in the background. Both levels of being are necessary for a full human life. I run into difficulties when I attempt to leave one mode of presence totally out.

I may be accustomed to living only on the level of the practical management of life, of human relationships, ideas, and feelings. I may try to deal also with my spiritual life as if it were merely another kind of business or science to be handled on the level of intelligent management. In the West, people are inclined to do just that.

Spirituality has suffered a decline in the West. In many instances it has been replaced by a quasi-spirituality. People lost contact with their deepest self. They tried to live their relationship to God and others merely on a pragmatic level or perhaps on the level of need and sentiment.

Man as spirit experiences a natural at-oneness with God, humanity, cosmos, and nature. Man as a managing person must temporarily abstract things out of this deeper at-oneness. He has to distance himself in order to discern clearly the practical differences between himself and others. Only then can he manage these differences and organize them in view of his practical projects.

It would not do to be only aware of my at-oneness with people and nature while driving my car. I must then be aware of the concrete practical differences between me, seated in the steel shell of my car, and the weak and vulnerable body of my fellow man crossing the street. We are spiritually at-one, surely, but also concretely different and I had best take this difference into account if I want to prevent an accident.

Western culture has mastered and refined the art of management of reality to the utmost. It is a technical and scientific culture; it builds great abstract theologies and philosophies; it masters techniques of mass production and performance. This massive conceptual and technical achievement contributed tremendously to the development of civilization. This stand of my culture, however, has inclined men of the West to experience themselves more as isolated managers manipulating nature and one another than as people basically at-one with each other, with God, and with nature.

This view understandably affected religion and led to a falsification of the spiritual life. Many saw themselves as isolated managers who had to interact with an equally isolated God, a kind of super-manager. He became in their mind separated from people, culture, and nature. As a mere manager, I cannot experience myself as one with God, fellow man, and nature. I am more likely to see myself as an isolated individual over and against equally isolated events, people, and things. I become preoccupied with make-believe problems about how to relate God, myself, and others to one another. My ego-intelligence starts to construe complex theories. I reason about vertical relationships to God and horizontal relationships to man. Should I find the horizontal relationship by first concentrating on the vertical? Is the vertical relationship implied in the horizontal? Should I first go to the isolated God? Should I then by logical reasonings find that somehow He is also related to my fellow men?

Such reasonings are endless. They will never satisfy. They are about quasi-problems. Such problems can only emerge in a culture which has lost contact with its original spiritual experience. People in such a culture are alienated from their deepest self. There is only one answer: make the leap from mere organizational living to spiritual living. Learn to live also on the deepest self level. Experience the oneness of world, man, and nature in the Divine Ground.

*Figure and Ground*

At the moment of prayer in solitude, I do not find only an isolated God. When working for my neighbor, I do not find only isolated fellow men. As a spiritual person, I find both God and my fellow men in my prayer as well as in my labors of love. There is a difference in intensity, however, between the experience of God in my hour of prayer and the experience of God during work with my fellow men. In turn, I experience my fellow man differently during my hour of prayer than during my attempts to respond to his needs. The difference between these two experiences can be explained in terms of the relationship between "figure" and "ground."

For example, I look at the painting by Rembrandt entitled *The Night Watch*. I focus on its harmony and composition. At the same time, I am aware of the human figures that make up this harmony of lines, light, and shadow. In this case the total composition is in the foreground of my awareness. The human persons are the background against which I see the "figure" of the composition as a whole; what is "figure," however, can become ground and what is ground can become figure. A moment later, I may be interested in the little drummer in the foreground. I see him emerging from the interplay of forms and colors.

In both cases, I am aware of the unity of the painting as a whole. In the first instance, the total composition was in the foreground of my awareness. The various figures formed the background. The totality of the composition stands out as figure. The persons in the painting are a never absent background. Against that background, I experience the totality of the composition as the foreground that dominates my awareness. I shift my attention from the total composition to the drummer. He emerges in the foreground of my awareness as figure. His appearance is sustained by the background of the composition as a whole.

This comparison may serve to illumine the life of prayer. I find God in solitude. I do not find an isolated deity met by an isolated I. Neither do I engage in cumbersome acrobatics of my managing mind. I do not remind myself anxiously of all that I have met outside my hour of prayer. I do not force myself at this moment of prayer to relate people and events in their particularity as isolated entities to an isolated God. All of this sounds strange to the spiritual man.

In my solitude on the level of the spirit, I never meet an isolated I or an isolated God or isolated others to be artificially and logically related to the Divine. I meet, in and through Christ, the Father. Implicitly, I meet all that the Father in love lets be and that the Son came to redeem. The Christian living a spiritual life experiences in the Father the basically holy or sacred nature of all that is. All flows forth from God Himself as the infinite and mysterious Origin of creation. During my hour of prayer, God's creation as a whole stands in the foreground of my awareness; its particular details become an ever present background.

As a Christian spiritual man, however, I must return from my solitude to everyday life. Then particular persons and things come into the foreground of my awareness. This does not mean that now the love of the Father is totally absent from my awareness. It is no longer in the foreground of my attention, but it lingers on as an ever present background. In and through Christ, the Father makes all particular persons and things be. He sustains them in creative love and compassion.

Just as the plain little drummer becomes meaningful against the background of the artist's creative composition, so the life of my fellow men becomes mysteriously meaningful against the background of God's creative love. This explains why as a spiritual man, I do not get fixated on some of my fellow men to the exclusion of others. Were I to identify exclusively with one or the other person or group, I would regress to some form of isolation. I would stand with one ego or a group of egos, with whom I identify, over against other egos, in whom I am not interested. I would be back on the level of religion as mere management.

Prayer in solitude serves to restore the primordial union between God, myself, all men, nature, and culture. This experience of original oneness is a necessary condition for meeting any concrete other, event, or thing in God or for meeting God or Christ in them.

# III
## SOLITUDE AND COMMUNION

Inner solitude is a precious condition for at-homeness with myself and for intimacy with God and men. Take as an example the life of Anne Frank. Her book, *The Diary of a Young Girl,* was written in seclusion from the outside world. It shows her communion with God and with the best aspirations of people everywhere.

When the diary was published, some readers raised a doubt as to whether a young girl like Anne could speak so profoundly to the human situation. There was even a suspicion that her diary might have been written by someone else. But, as the records show, it was her own work, not meant for publication but simply to get hold of her own experience. The book has since proved to be a success in many languages. The movie and theater play based upon it attract crowds wherever they are produced.

History imposed on this girl unusual conditions—some of which are found only in the life of people who come together to live as contemplative monks or nuns.

To escape the danger of imprisonment by the Nazis, she had to hide with her family and a few acquaintances in a few rooms on the top floors of an old warehouse in Amsterdam. This seclusion took her suddenly away from her involvement with the children and adults of her school and neighborhood. From the first pages of the diary and from later witnesses who knew her, we know that Anne had been exuberantly involved in this familiar world. She was, as she herself admits, a real chatterbox, always on the go.

Cut off from her social life, she begins to experience herself and her fellow men in a new way. The collision all day long with a few persons, irritated and vulnerable under the constant threat of imprisonment and death, compels her to reflect on herself in relation to each one of them. This reflection makes her discover her uniqueness; it throws her back in inner solitude.

She makes this inner aloneness meaningful and even deepens it by withdrawing time and again from the few people around her. She tries to find a corner of her own where she can be by herself. Sometimes she climbs to the attic. In solitude she can look through the window over the rooftops of the city. At such moments, she is able to find in herself the sufferings, needs, and longings she has in common with all men. In solitary self-presence—sometimes implicitly, sometimes explicitly before God—she becomes present to all of us. She speaks about things we recognize as common to our own moments of self-comprehension.

Separation from friends and neighbors, from school and environment, silence in the sense of not making any noise—these new experiences are thrust upon her. All day long people are working on the lower floors of the same building where she and her family are hiding. They may not betray their presence, not even by coughing, to these employees. This forced silence was more cruel than separation. However, in Anne's case, silence as well as inner solitude foster a remarkable growth. Her diary records in a moving way the awakening of herself as a spiritual person.

Anne Frank found in solitude her innermost originality. She discovered herself as originating from God in her uniqueness—as the origin of spiritual experiences and aspirations. At the same time she became aware of others in their most intimate reality. How could this be? How could this young girl —inwardly alone and in silence—be at the same time so at-one with herself and all men?

## Commonality of Spiritual Experience

Everyone is called to the life of the spirit, yet each person has to discover this life in his own way. I have to experience uniquely what is common to all. At some moment I, like Anne, may become aware of my call to solitude. I see my life in a new light. I notice what can foster or impede my original unfolding. I sense that spiritual enlightenment grants insight not only into the spiritual dimension of my self. It elucidates indirectly other aspects of human life.

Fundamentally the dynamics of inward living are the same for all people. I cannot understand these dynamics merely by observing their effects on the life of others. Only personal experience reveals their meaning in such a way that I can make it my own. These universal dynamics, when experienced anew, can bring me back to the core of my self. This is what happened to Anne Frank.

She writes about her experience of inwardness. She tells us what is disclosed to her in inner solitude. This is why her diary can speak to all of us who have experienced something similar. It can also speak to those of us who are ready for the discovery of the fundamental structures of the spiritual life, even if we may not yet live these dynamics ourselves.

The story of Anne Frank and its appeal helps to explain the universal appeal of spiritual writers like John of the Cross, Teresa of Avila, Francis Libermann, Jeremy Taylor, John Donne, Confucius and Lao-Tze. They tell their own experiences; yet they appeal to people of all times, of all religions, and of all cultures.

The spiritual masters of various backgrounds display many similarities as long as they are speaking about the fundamental dynamics of the spiritual life. They differ, of course, when they tell us how these dynamics are personally lived in light of the particular influence of their own religion, culture, temperament, and history.

These writers, like Anne Frank, discover their deepest commonality with others by retreating in solitude. There is no other way given to man to discover the spiritual reality he shares with his fellow men. The more I close myself from myself as spirit, the more removed I will be from the other in his deepest reality. It may happen that I never meet myself as spirit. Then I can never expect to interact with others on more than a superficial plane. I may meet them merely as a smooth socializer, a religious or social do-gooder, or a quasi-apostolic busybody.

## Crowd and Collectivity

You may ask, "What about everyday life?" It is one thing to speak about inner solitude in order to commune with others as spirit. But does not everyday life imply more than communing on this level?

In everyday life we can distinguish three kinds of togetherness: that of crowd, that of collectivity, and that of spirit. Togetherness is human when communion of spirit prevails over that of crowd and collectivity. We say *prevail*, for human togetherness can never be strictly spiritual; it always implies certain aspects of crowd and collective behavior.

Let us first consider the crowd. Crowd behavior can be traced to the fact that we are not only spiritual and practical persons; we are also vital. As such, we feel and sense things; we are moved by each other's emotions. Watching a champion baseball game, we feel aroused by the excitement that surges through the crowd. Something similar happens in other gatherings whenever emotional outbursts and enthusiastic behavior make us feel at-one with each other. There is nothing wrong with that as long as shared excitement does not become the main mark of all human togetherness.

Collectivity is another component of our everyday togetherness. This aspect can be traced to the fact that we are not merely spiritual and emotional persons. We are also practical and realistic. We feel urged to organize our common actions in such a way that spiritual ideals will have a noticeable effect on daily life. To organize our togetherness in practical and effective ways, we need collective structures of time and place, of dues and duties, of purposes and customs. Such collective structures are necessary, but they too can become harmful. Like crowd dynamics, they can take over to an unhealthy degree. Collective structures can block out personal and spiritual inspirations. They can be dehumanizing.

In daily life, we tend to become absorbed by common feelings and collective structures. We are always on the verge of allowing them to take over. This is true even for our loftiest endeavors. Social work, academic pursuits, apostolic actions, fights for justice are communal enterprises which necessarily have crowd aspects and collective features. The trouble is that these crowd sentiments and collective structures can become dominant. We may then forget what inspired our actions in the first place.

Our togetherness is threatened constantly by the oblivion of the spirit. We have to be called back from absorption in the crowd and collectivity dimensions of all communal behavior. This calling back can take place only in the individual. The appeals of the Spirit are heard not by the mass but by the person in his uniqueness. This is why each person needs to return from time to time to himself in solitude.

I need to distance myself periodically from the emotional and organizational aspects of my life with family, church, or organization. Solitude restores the spiritual dimension of my life with others and helps our everyday togetherness to remain human and spiritual. Prayerful recollection in silence and solitude is the best way to regain the spiritual Origin of our shared life with others.

## IV

## SPIRITUALITY AND MEDITATIVE REFLECTION

Spirituality means first of all my personal attempt to live a spiritual life. It may also refer to a systematic doctrine about spiritual living. When I say that it is not easy for me at this moment of my life to maintain the right conditions for my own life of prayer, I am speaking about spirituality in the first sense. For I speak only about my personal life here and now. When I compare the systematic doctrine of spirituality of the French School to the doctrine of Ignatius, I am occupied with spirituality in the second sense.

Spirituality can thus mean personal spiritual living or a theoretical systematic doctrine of spiritual life. There is still a third meaning to the word. Spirituality can indicate literary expressions of the spiritual life. These are not meant to be systematic treatises but coherent records of religious experience. They are written by persons who have tried to live a life of prayerful presence to the Divine. An example of such writing is found in the autobiography of Thérèse of Lisieux or in the diary of Dag Hammarskjöld.

I can participate in the efforts and experiences of these spiritual writers to the degree that I read their writings reflectively. Participation in such wisdom through meditative reflection is necessary if I am to grow spiritually. Such participation helps me to avoid certain pitfalls. It teaches me ways that may facilitate my own spiritual unfolding.

I may find it difficult to participate in the insights and experiences of the spiritual writer. Many people in our Western culture have lost the ability to participate reflectively in the experiential description the writer gives of the dynamics of spiritual living. Due to this loss, spiritual writing about religious experience has been less promoted than theological, social, and theoretical writing about religion. As much as we might wish it, there is no abundance of contemporary writing on the spiritual life. Fortunately, previous periods of history have graced humanity with a rich harvest of spiritual writing. How can I profit from this accumulated spiritual wisdom of mankind over the centuries?

## Expressions of the Spiritual Life

The life of the spirit has been lived by many people in various cultures and religions. Their wisdom can be beneficial to all. Many of them have written down the experience of their attempt to live a life wholly present to the Sacred. They describe the path they followed, the pitfalls they encountered, the consequences of their attempt.

A special attitude guides the spiritual writer. It could be called that of meditative or participative reflection. The writer reflects on what he himself experiences in his attempt to live the spiritual life. His reflection *participates in* his original experience. This participative attitude lends a living quality to his words. It invites participation in turn on the part of the reader. I profit most when I try to participate personally in the experience the writer communicates.

There are different kinds of reflection, of course. A theological writer may reflect on the relations that exist between the three persons of the Holy Trinity. His scholarly reflection is objective, analytic. He tries to make clear what these divine relations mean in terms of logical categories. Usually, he obtains such categories from a philosophical or theological system already in existence or in the process of formation. His reflection serves religion by satisfying the demands of man's analytical intelligence.

A quite different kind of reflection takes place when a person like Elizabeth of the Trinity describes her experience of living with the indwelling Divine Persons. Daily attempting to live in presence to the Trinity, she always discovers new depths of meaning. These depths are not the conclusions of abstract speculation. They are personal experiences of love for the Divine.

When I love someone, I am always discovering

# ON BEING YOURSELF

sides of him I never saw before. Likewise, in her love, Elizabeth reveals a new awareness of the holy intimacy which binds the Divine Persons; and she experiences how this intimacy extends to the smallest of creatures. It is this kind of awareness which she communicates in her writings that touches us.

## Scientific Attitude, Reflective Attitude

A good reader of spiritual writings attempts in turn to meditate reflectively on them. He participates, according to his uniqueness, in the experience they communicate. It may be difficult for me to understand what such participation means. My education tends to make me more familiar with the scientific attitude. I may feel more at home, for example, with the theologian than the spiritual writer. The attitude of reflective participation may be foreign to me. To get a clearer notion of this, compare the participative attitude of spiritual reading to the attitude involved in the study of scientific theology or the attitude of praying to the attitude of preparing for an exam.

A monk rises in the night to sing the Holy Office with his fellow monks. While chanting the sacred texts, he feels a quieting of his analytic intelligence taking place. Without this quieting, his restless mind might tempt him to feverishly relate these texts to the theological systems he has to study during the day as preparation for his ordination to the priesthood. Years of inner silence and discipline have

[ 50 ]

enabled him to bring himself, with God's Grace, to a point of quietude. His analytic mind comes to rest. Room is left now for presence to God. Even in times of "spiritual drought," he is careful not to let his mind wander off in scientific analyses and intellectual explanations of the texts he chants. On the contrary, he knows that he has to wait in emptiness. God should find him ready to be filled when He speaks to him, as may happen, in and through the psalms and texts recited in the choir.

Contrast this attitude with the one the same monk must adopt during the day when he studies theological texts to prepare for his exam. The professor will ask him about various theoretical concepts. He presupposes that the student monk will use his analytical intelligence for explication and reconstruction. The monk knows, therefore, that silencing his scientific mind at exam time would in effect make it impossible for him to understand the conceptual systems he has to explain to his examiners. His attitude of mind must now be different from the attitude of meditative dwelling which was his in the choir.

Differentiation of attitudes is unavoidable in human life. I cannot be all things at all times. The necessity of differentiation need not cause a split in my personality, however. In this example, the monk is made whole by his intention to do the Will of the Father. God simply asks him to be a contemplative in the choir, a student of scientific theology when preparing for an exam. The theological reflection, typical of the monk as student, and the participative reflection, typical of the monk as contemplative, are both necessary in the respective situations described.

Scientific and meditative reflection mutually illumine one another; but one is not reducible to the other. This holds true not only for monks but for every person on the way toward a spiritual life. Each person should foster the art of an original "dwelling participation" in the holy texts of his religion. As the situation demands, he may be asked to develop at other times the attitude of a more scientific reflection.

# V

# SPIRITUALITY AND PSYCHOLOGY

Originality in the realm of the spirit is a losing of myself in the Origin of all that is, in the Ground of my being, in God. In losing myself, I find my true self at its very Center. I return, as it were, to the Origin of all origins. I experience everything as welling up from that Ground, my unique self included. I feel like a modulation, a ripple on the stream of all that He allows to be. I forget my anxious concern for absolute ego security. I am most near to and most identified with the Eternal Origin that makes me be in a unique way and calls me forth as nothing else is called forth in this cosmos.

As long as I try willfully to be myself only on the level of person and culture, I am still the victim of cultural pressures and personal passions. They obscure the Source of my uniqueness. When I banish my preoccupation about being a person, I am most near to being one: "Whoever tries to preserve his life will lose it; whoever loses it will keep it" (Luke 17:33).

## ON BEING YOURSELF

### *Problem of Spiritual Living in Western Culture*

A certain style of personal and cultural living can prepare me for this life of centering in the Divine. Such living is most simply the incarnation of the spiritual life in my daily endeavors. Spirituality in the most profound sense resides in the core of my being, in my deepest self or spirit, where I as willing unite my will to the Will of God for me. Whatever I learn, do or observe should lead me to this core; daily life in turn should be an outflow of this center. My self as seeking, thinking, feeling should become increasingly an incarnation of my unique original presence to God in the core of my being. In no way should I separate the vital, cultural, and personal dimensions of my self from the spiritual. I may distinguish these dimensions but I must not separate them. The vital, personal, cultural, and spiritual dimensions of my self should flow together as an harmonious whole.

Unfortunately, I am inclined to separate one dimension from the other. I often live the vital, cultural, or personal side of my self in isolation from the spiritual. A whole culture in fact can promote a spiritless existence. In that case, mere theology, behavioristic and ego-psychologies may take precedence over the wisdom of spirituality. Theology and the human sciences are important for certain aspects of my development, but they can never take the place of spirituality.

Western culture especially seems alienated from the dynamics of the life of the spirit; it is inclined to reduce the dynamics of the spirit to those of the integrating ego and superego. The latter dynamics are studied by psychology, psychiatry, sociology, and other human sciences. Time is needed to remedy this deficiency. Unfortunately, our ignorance has become so great we hardly know where to begin.

## Role of Psychology

The dynamics of spirituality are not the same as the dynamics of psychology. Psychology and psychiatry as developed in Western culture, do not speak about the dynamics of the spirit. They omit these important dimensions from their consideration. The psyche studied is thus a "decapitated" psyche. Psychology and psychiatry have developed worthwhile considerations about behavior, adaptations to the environment, development of cultural and personal potentialities, the integration of the person on the levels of ego and superego, human encounter, and self-actualization. Some of these studies may foster an understanding of certain *conditions for* a spiritual life. Such understanding, however, is not yet an insight into the spiritual life itself. Some psychiatrists or psychologists may have dealt lightly with the dynamics of the spirit, but such cases are few and far between. Often the scientist concerned was considered a "maverick" out of touch with his special field.

The reasons for this are not far to seek. The methods to be used in the study of the spiritual dimension of the self differ from those to be used for the study of the measurable aspects of the vital, cultural, and personal dimensions of this same self. Western scientific man has been inclined to identify the methods of the latter study as the only valid ones—valid because more measurable. The study of fundamental spirituality was on this basis eliminated for the most part from the realm of the social sciences.

Fortunately, mankind had gathered a wealth of knowledge about the life of the spirit before the rise of social sciences. The art and discipline of spirituality is one of the oldest, if not the oldest, of human disciplines. We are not speaking now of the various theologies about spirituality or a series of courses in the history of spirituality. We mean specifically the study of the fundamental dynamics of the spirit itself. This study goes back to the beginnings of the cultural history of mankind. It has been preserved in scrolls, monuments, and books written in many languages.

## Man as Manager and Man as Spirit

The study of the dynamics of spirituality is not included in the present day psychological study of man. We are referring here to the scientific understanding of psychology as it currently dominates the cultural scene. To illustrate this exclusion, we may compare again the difference between man as manager and man as spirit.

What are the dynamics of man as manager or ego as formulated by current social sciences? What are those of the spirit as contained in the records of spirituality? What is the difference between them?

Let us say that by all current standards I am integrated, well-adapted, and effective vitally, culturally, and on the levels of ego and superego. I am an active, organized person, able to plan things well. I am disciplined, regulated, explorative, analytical. All of these attributes are necessary for full human living. To some degree, they are necessary for the spiritual life. Without some integration, without some organization of my feelings and attitudes, of my human relationships, environment, task, and religious behavior, I cannot live on the level of the spirit.

Such integration as a person who can manage well implies that I grow in self-esteem, that I make myself an effective force in my environment, that I meet others humanly, that I control my emotions, that I build my career, that I develop some philosophical, theological, and ethical view of life in which each thing falls into place. The human sciences too may help me in my attempt to build up such a disciplined personality in control of myself and in effective interaction with my environment. A well-laid foundation of self-discipline, self-understanding, and social efficiency facilitates in turn a free and safe surrender to the dynamics of the spirit.

I can view these ego-dynamics from the perspective of scientific psychology. I can also look at them in the light of spirituality. Much ego-psychology seems to make these dynamics, this ego-building, an end in itself. This very view affects the nature of these dynamics. If I live the limited immediate aims of such psychological structures *as ultimate,* I cannot integrate them within the life of the spirit. On the other hand, in light of the spirit, I can value and foster these dynamics as necessary ego-functions. I see them as insuring the emergence and maintenance of facilitating conditions for the life of the spirit. But I do not make the building of my ego the ultimate aim of my life.

Let us look again at the spiritual life of Dag Hammarskjöld. We can compare his diary entries about the spiritual life with his effective functioning as Secretary-General of the United Nations. There is a mutual influence of one on the other. He reached a high integration of both spirituality and ego-functionality. His union with the Lord inspired him to function efficiently. His spirituality increased his ego-functionality. But he did not make ego-functioning the ultimate aim and meaning of his life.

In the realm of the spirit, my primordial concern is not for self-enhancement or mere ego-fulfillment but for awareness of my nothingness before the mystery of the Sacred. The main attempt is not to be socially active all the time but to live also in solitude. Not to make myself felt but to be humble and forgotten. Not to make ultimate the building of a career and the planning of a future but to surrender to the mystery of my Origin. Not to know but to live in the cloud of unknowing.

In regard to my true ultimate aims, the dynamics of my spiritual life complement those of my psychological life. Both kinds of dynamics ideally form a unity in diversity. The dynamics of the spirit should complement and purify the dynamics of the ego and the body. This is why a master of initiation into spirituality needs to know much more than psychology. He should have the wisdom to take in this perspective and ultimately surpass it. Otherwise, he may confine the initiates under his care merely to the level of ego and superego development. He may preach only an ego-religion or a quasi-spirituality, perhaps adorned with some abstract theology but never coming to the heart and center of the spiritual life.

# VI
## ORIGINAL PRAYER

My prayer should be true to who I am. I may meet people who find a popular style of prayer that means a lot to them. They may press me to join their movement. They may chide my style of prayer as too simple, too old fashioned. I may give up what works for me and end up with no prayer at all. For their popular way may not be my way.

Ted, a graduate student, talked to me recently about his experience with prayer. "I read somewhere," he said, "that Dag Hammarskjöld meditated daily on the *Imitation of Christ.* They say the book was in his pocket when he died in an air crash. I bought myself a copy of the *Imitation.* From time to time, I would read a few sentences. They made me think. And believe it or not, helped me to pray."

"Splendid," I said. "You discovered the art of meditative reading and learned to appreciate a spiritual classic. That this little book meant a lot to Hammarskjöld is beside the point. That it means a lot to you is the crucial thing. Be wise enough to follow your attraction. Grace moves different people in dif-

ferent ways. Every man should be grateful for anything that makes life more meaningful for him, no
matter what others like or dislike."

Ted turned to me and said, "Not everyone seems
to think that way. A young theology teacher in my
college disapproves of the *Imitation*. The book makes
you too 'individualistic,' he says. He warned me
against what he called the 'Jesus and I' syndrome. It
sounded like a disease. 'Modern people,' he said, 'pray
to the Cosmic Christ and to God as the hidden
Ground of their being.'

"I was impressed by him and when I felt the need
to pray, I tried to address myself to Christ in the
cosmos or to talk to the hidden Ground of my being.
But it felt funny—talking to my ground."

Ted gave up on prayer. Still he wanted to pray. He
did not dare to pick up the *Imitation* again. He did
not want to look old-fashioned. Not even to himself.

Many fine intellectuals are moved by the theory of
the evolution of man and the cosmos. An impressive
theory like that can become a way of life for some
people. These same people may love Christ. They
want to find His Presence in everything that means
much to them. Understandably, they want Christ
present in their view of the cosmos. What results is
the idea of the Cosmic Christ. They feel at home with
this image. They can pray to Christ in the cosmos.
No one would deny how splendid it is that they have
found their personal way to the Lord. But they
should not impose this way on others, whose unique-

ness may differ from theirs.

Other people find that feeling of homecoming in a philosophical view of life. The word "being" is no longer abstract to them. Thinking about God as the Ground of their being helps them to pray. It ties in with their originality, but it does not necessarily work for others.

A girl told me about her original prayer: "I like to slip into church or chapel. It's nice and quiet. Nobody else is there. I look at the tabernacle. He is there. He sees me. He cares. I talk to Him, and I feel comforted. But friends told me that people who are with it these days find God in interpersonal relationships. They warned me that I should be more up to date. I listened to them and when I felt like praying, I no longer went to the chapel. I tried to pray to Christ as present in interpersonal relationships. I always ended up being distracted by the words and manners of the people with whom I ate dinner, talked, or danced. Then I forgot that I was supposed to pray to Christ in them."

Many intellectuals today have discovered that having human relationships is more important than just reading about them in books. Intellectuals spend a lot of time in libraries and classrooms, behind desks, and at scholarly conventions. They may forget about the goodness of simple contacts with people. When they discover this anew, they become excited.

Being intellectuals, they are apt to build theories about their rediscovery of human relationships. They write books and articles, form discussion groups and encounter teams. At the center of their view of the world, they now place their newly discovered interpersonal relationships. At the same time they want Christ also to be at the heart of their lives and thought. No wonder they try to find Him now in the mystery of human encounter.

Such encounter happens to be the current center of their concern. This kind of prayer ties in with the stage of original unfolding they find themselves in at this moment of their lives. Others, however, cannot get excited about evolution, interpersonal relationships, and the Ground of their being. If they feel like praying, they simply talk to the Lord as a friend or a brother. Some intellectuals say, "Not good enough ... it's the 'Jesus and I' syndrome." What do we do?

It's important to be relaxed about the whole thing. We live in a climate of change and discovery. Intellectuals are eager to develop new ideas. Each new idea may be an aspect of the truth. For example, a theologian may elaborate in a new theology the notion that Christ is also present in the cosmos. It may be worthwhile to hear or read about his theology. It is interesting to know how different people in our culture make different aspects of reality central in accordance with their initial or expanding originality. It is even more interesting to see how they try to relate a new insight to the truth of Revelation. Never should we confuse such exploratory theologies with

the essential doctrine of the Church and with spirituality.

Essential Church doctrine is what any Catholic, no
matter what his originality, should believe if he wants
to stay a Catholic. For example, he must believe as an
essential teaching of the Church that God became
man in Christ. Theologies can be speculations on or
elaborations of essential teachings of the Church. For
example, a theology can center itself around the
question, "Does the Incarnation imply a special mode
of presence of Christ in the cosmos?" The discipline
or study of fundamental spirituality is something else
again. It is an operational discipline in that it tells me
how the essential truths of the Church can operate or
work in my own life in such a way that I as a unique
person can become more at-one with my Lord.

God is present everywhere. He is immanent and
transcendent. He is the Ground of my being and the
completion of it. He is in my office or living room
but His Presence also pervades the cosmos. I can find
Him in myself and in the other, in solitude, and in
interpersonal relationships, in Church teaching, scrip-
ture, and sacraments.

The Lord may choose a book like the *Imitation* to
show Himself to Hammarskjöld, a chapel to speak to
somebody else, the mystery of evolution to manifest
Himself to a student of biology, the beauty of human
encounter to reveal Himself to a person who special-
izes in counseling or social work. Nobody can arbi-
trarily choose in what way he wants to pray. It

depends on the original make-up God has given him and on the unique unfolding of this given originality in the light of the particular graces and successive life situations God has exposed him to.

Each person should graciously comply with the limited way in which the Lord deigns to give Himself to him. He chooses the way, not we. Thus I must never prefer a worthwhile way of prayer for others to His way for me. It simply will not work. I cannot tell the Lord how to manifest Himself to me.

## Theological Speculation and Original Prayer

The serpent in the paradise story suggested that eating a fruit of a certain tree would magically grant man divine consciousness. We may try something like that with the "fruits of the trees" of theologies, human sciences, social actions, sensitivity training. All these fruits can be excellent, but not for all people at all times in all situations. Only God in His own good time decides what fruit of what tree will be the avenue by which He will manifest Himself to me as a unique person in a certain period of my life.

Another student related to me the following incident: "Last semester," he said, "we had a visiting theologian teaching on our campus. He gave a talk on man's relationship to the Divine. It was pretty complex. He spoke about a vertical and a horizontal relationship to the Infinite. He seemed in favor of the horizontal; but somehow in the horizontal you could find the vertical and in the vertical the horizontal and so on.

"I probably mixed it all up. When I felt like praying I tried it out: horizontal-vertical, vertical-horizontal. I felt like a religious acrobat. I got all confused and ended up with a headache.

"Now I see what I did wrong. I gave this theological speculation the same status as an essential doctrine of the Church, which I should believe and follow no matter how I feel personally. Moreover, I listened to the theologian as if he were my personal spiritual guide, who knew me well and could tell me how I should personally pray best. To top it all off, I used the horizontal-vertical formula as a magic wand; it *would* lead me to the right, religious experience *if only* I worked at it hard enough."

The lesson this student learned is simply this: don't confuse theological speculation with spirituality. Be interested in the speculations of theologians. You are not only called to live a meaningful spiritual life; you are also asked to be a man of culture, a man with a well developed speculative intelligence. Speculative theology can help you to develop the theological dimension of your intelligence, but be clear that this development *may* or *may not* be helpful to your personal life of prayer.

# VII
# FAITH, BELIEF, AND ORIGINALITY

Many people
write on the social aspect of religion. They propose
goals and methods that can improve society, family,
and community. They give their readers something to
believe in even if their proposals do not work immediately. Many people feel the need to share such beliefs.
They want to believe in political demonstrations,
slum clearance, cessation of war, collegiality, ecology,
woman's liberation, renewal of institutions, political
projects of social betterment, and many worthwhile
causes. Such beliefs give meaning to their daily lives
and make them feel relevant in a complex and confused society crying out for salvation.

The life of the spirit, the original life of faith, can
express itself in a variety of social beliefs, some of
which may or may not tie in with my originality.

For my personal life, social beliefs are not of
ultimate importance in themselves. In isolation, social
beliefs may even be harmful for my original growth.

I may believe wholeheartedly in my projects for
social betterment. I share the life of the poor, picket,

and participate in demonstrations for social justice. I am convinced that only methods like this will make Christianity relevant and lead to change in the world. I may even feel that religion can be meaningful only insofar as it helps people to make actual such social beliefs.

Social beliefs and the actions they evoke may help me to suffer with others, but do they really make me one with them in the deepest sense? Should there not be something more original in my self and others that goes deeper than social beliefs alone, something that does not exclude these beliefs but sustains and nourishes them? Deeper than social beliefs is faith and I have to be sure that my enthusiastic beliefs are not taking the place of faith.

As soon as I extol my beliefs as *ultimate,* I become in effect irrelevant to the most original needs of myself and others. Isolated beliefs cannot take the place of faith, which rests in the Divine Ground underlying all that is. Such a statement may upset me. Why? Perhaps because my beliefs may have already taken such an absolute place in my life that I can think only in opposing terms. I say to myself, "Either my beliefs are absolutely right or yours are absolutely wrong. Take them as they are or don't take them at all." I cannot listen to the other side if I have staked my future on the belief that what I am doing for society is the only thing that makes sense and gives meaning to life. This attitude is no longer one of belief; belief has become a substitute for faith.

## Faith, Belief, and Originality

I may resent the suggestion that over, above, and under my belief there should be some attitude more original, more essential, more comprehensive. It scares me to think that my cherished beliefs may be relative after all. Like all men, I too live in doubt, anxiety, and confusion. I too try to relieve my anxiety by searching for some final solution to the uncertainties of life. However, I should not try to find the final solution for life's problems in social belief alone.

Unfortunate for my peace of mind, but fortunate for my possibility of inner growth, I know at some level that my social beliefs cannot be the panacea for all ills or give lasting meaning to life. I may have tried to block out the uncertainties, the gnawing doubts that make me nervous and afraid. It is not easy for me to hold onto my social beliefs and at the same time acknowledge their limitations. If it were a simple matter of making light of my social commitment and forgetting it, fine. But to admit that my involvement is valuable, to be delighted with my belief, and at the same time not to regard it as ultimate is another thing. Nonetheless, this is what I must do. Faith tells me that ultimately my social belief is provisional and temporal.

Perhaps other Christians admire me for the outstanding social work I am doing. It may be all right for them to admire me, but it would be wrong for them to see in my social beliefs the *essence* of my Christianity. I could find the same or perhaps a better social belief and action outside of my religion. The essence of Christianity is faith in Christ as God and Savior. One of the many fruits of that faith may be admirable social belief and action.

As a Christian, I must live in the world. I must participate in the culture. Therefore, I must participate in one or the other belief in tune with my unique make-up and original life calling.

Christian faith in the creation and redemption of the world, in the presence of Christ in my fellow man, inspires me to participation. This same faith prevents a blind enslavement to any particular social movement or viewpoint. There are many changing social, political, and cultural beliefs. Each one of them is relative, but some may persist in making them absolute. Insensitively, such people try to enlist everyone in their special social movement without reverence for each person's unique calling.

For this reason, Christian spirituality likes to put each social and cultural belief in perspective. It enables the truly faithful man, the man "full of faith," to decide in profound liberty what belief fits his originality and his life situation best at this moment. His faith inspires him to the kind of belief that seems most in tune with his personality, life history, and educational background, and with the potential contribution he can make to humanity.

Every human being, Christian or not, needs both faith and beliefs. They are part of man's nature. Faith is not the prerogative of any religion. It is an attitude of trust in the original meaningfulness of life, even when beliefs are shattered. Faith in life, nature, or humanity helps me to survive the destruction of time-bound beliefs. Faith grants me the courage I need to express my basic trust in ever new beliefs. All faith inevitably points to religious faith and obtains its deepest significance in the specific religion like Christianity.

## A Personal Account of This Point

I discussed this matter of faith and belief with a group of people. One sister who was there said to me:

"I am beginning to see what you mean. Recently I participated in a series of renewal meetings in my religious congregation. I was elected a member of several committees. We proposed many exciting things: We should be relevant to humanity in a new way; we should reach the people by change in dress and custom; we should build the ideal community among ourselves, open, loving, and affectionate. I seldom felt so enthusiastic in my life. Still at quiet moments some uneasiness crept in. Things were going fine. Everyone was so alive—new ideas, new beliefs, new projects were popping up among the excited delegates.

"Now I realize why a deep-down uneasiness kept emerging too. The beliefs of our renewal chapter were probably good and commendable. But they were proposed and defended with an almost fanatic conviction. Some of us almost seemed to say that only the triumph of these beliefs would justify the continuation of religious life itself. We seemed to stake not only our own lives but the life of the whole community on the fulfillment of those beliefs. Indeed, for some of us they seemed to take the place of faith.

"I never understood before why some priests, brothers, sisters, laymen—so admired for their social beliefs—could suddenly fall away from their faith. Now I see that in some instances their beliefs may have been stronger than their faith. Often disappointed in their beliefs or resenting opposition to them by fellow Christians, they no longer had a deep personal life of faith to fall back upon. I can see now that our religious congregations can only survive if they nourish in their members the life of faith without neglecting the nourishment of beliefs that should be sustained by that faith."

Sister's experience speaks to us all. We all are in danger of losing our bearings if we try to live by beliefs alone. We need a faith that sustains and surpasses these beliefs. Such fundamental faith creates and maintains room for our original unfolding. Social beliefs are bound to specific times, situations, and temperaments. If they become absolute, they necessarily cramp our original life style as well as the style of those on whom we impose our beliefs by means of social pressure or by the seduction of enthusiasm.

# VIII

## JUDGMENT AND RESPECT OF ORIGINALITY

A president of
a company once told me, "The Lord tells us not to
judge our fellow men. But if I do not sit in judgment,
my company may promote the wrong people. President and stockholders will be upset; personnel will be
unhappy; production will go down; and I may be
fired."

Not long ago, I spoke to a novice mistress who
complained: "I have to judge all day long. I have to
judge what some of my novices are doing. I have to
judge whether the priests and sisters who want to
address them are fit or unfit for speaking wisely to
them. Even though I know I have to judge all these
people, somehow I feel it is not right."

It is clear that daily life is impossible without some
kind of judgment. Without judgment, a person could
not be a good vice-president, or a directress of
novices, or a responsible mother. The counsel not to
judge others means that we should not judge their
original personality or original guilt.

A person can be guilty only in so far as he is

responsible for his acts. My responsibility or "ability to respond" is limited by my original make-up. My biochemical, vital, psychological, and spiritual originality sets the limits of the behavior I can be totally responsible for and therefore guilty of. Nobody knows for sure the original limits of a person. That is why the spiritual man tries to avoid an *ultimate* judgment about the original responsibility of another. His is a *practical* judgment.

God gives us a task to do. The task demands that we judge whether or not other people can help us fulfill our mission. Say that someone is an alcoholic. A president clearly cannot put him in charge of the personnel of his company as long as he cannot cope with his alcoholism. But the president does not judge the original moral guilt of the man. He leaves that to the Lord. Only the Lord knows the extenuating circumstances in his background. He alone knows the good will of this alcoholic—the way he struggles with his problem and sanctifies himself in this struggle. He alone knows the limits of spiritual originality to which this person is called.

The spiritual man is always ready to believe that he himself would be far worse off, were it not for the Grace of God, that he himself is probably below this man in the eyes of the Father. Charity and humility permeate the practical judgment of the spiritual man. If necessary he communicates his judgment to this person or others with respect and humility. He does not judge this man as an original person; he judges only the impracticality of having a man with these difficulties operating in this specific practical situation.

A mother came to see me and said, "My difficulty is that I tend to become harsh in the judgment of my children. I am probably scared of what the neighbors may say about their clothing or long hair."

What the neighbors say may be a practical thing to consider in certain neighborhoods. Their opinions should be taken into account to some degree. I reminded her, "When you feel yourself becoming harsh, you may ask if the main source of your anger is that you are afraid that you and your family may look less neat and respectable in the eyes of your neighbors. In that case your judgment may not be permeated by the charity and humility of our Lord. It may be hardened by self-preoccupation."

She answered: "There is another reason why I feel guilty about judging my children. Sometimes I feel that I become inflexible in my opinions. I close myself up within my own ideas. I am not willing to see that things have changed and that my judgment should change too. As a result, I sometimes lose contact with my kids. When I am that way, it is also difficult to pray. I feel isolated in my pride and stubbornness, closed off from the Divine Light that shines forth in changing people and situations."

Inflexibility and stubbornness of judgment may inhibit the life of the Spirit. They prevent the free functioning of my own original sensitivity. They paralyze also original spontaneity in others. The Spirit of the Lord is one of flexible openness to the manifestations of the Will of the Father in every changing situation and original person. It is not enough that we refrain from passing ultimate judgment on the original guilt of our fellow men. Nor is it enough that we prevent the hardening of our judgment by self-centered motives. Our practical everyday judgment must be humbly experienced as finite and in danger of error, in need of change and development.

You may say: "How can I judge firmly, knowing that my insight may be different ten years from now?"

Spiritual life implies the humble acceptance that we know relatively little about the original calling of others and yet that we still have to judge and act courageously by the light given to us within a situation. We should keep our judgments open for change and development. In the meantime, we have to judge people practically in the limited light that is granted to us.

The spiritual person accepts that his light is limited. He is only on the way to wisdom. If he would not judge and act at all, he would remove himself from the daily world. While seeking to expand his insight by prayer, consultation, reading, reflection, he still has to judge and act practically. Otherwise, other forces will wrench life away from him and from the influence of Christ which he tries to represent. The man who refuses to make practical

*Judgment and Respect of Originality*

judgments isolates his spiritual life from the incarnation of Christ in the culture.

What if the judgment of the spiritual man is wrong in spite of his prayer, study, consultation, and reflection? I may honestly think that a man is not good for a certain position in my company. A novice master may be convinced that a novice should be sent home. A mother may feel sure that her children should not go to a certain place at night. What if they are wrong?

The man of faith knows that in spite of his best efforts some of his judgments will be faulty. The original calling of others may escape his insight. He knows also that the Divine Will may allow this blindness. He believes deeply that nothing happens outside the mysterious Presence of Providence. In faith he accepts that things may result from his faulty judgment which seem meaningless from the viewpoint of human wisdom but may be made meaningful in light of Divine Wisdom.

Even though we ought to limit ourselves to practical judgments, why is it that we fall easily into angry emotional and moral judgments?

There are many reasons for this. Let me mention only one. Not living in the faith that even a mistaken judgment can be meaningful in the light of Divine Wisdom, we lack the strength to act on our practical judgments. To overcome this indecision, we work ourselves into an emotional pitch. We begin to tell ourselves and others how mean and immoral the person is whom we want to fire or send home. Before we know it, we begin to judge the person's original guilt.

When we come together with colleagues and talk about an unpleasant employee, we sometimes allow our emotions to take over. Before we realize what we are doing, we cut him to pieces. At the end of the conversation, it seems clear that he is not even a decent human being.

We may gossip about a wife in the neighborhood whom we have seen with another man. We make up theories about her life and usually end up condemning her.

We are always tempted to become uncharitable and absolute in our judgments. We are prone to vibrate with the angry emotions of others. Spiritual life implies an inner zone of silence and recollection, where we can be our spiritual selves. This zone of quiet helps us to recognize the moment we become emotionally contaminated by the outbursts of other people against a person we dislike. With the Grace of our Lord, we can then try to calm our emotions before they seduce us into making an ultimate moral judgment about the original guilt of this person.

## IX

## SPIRITUAL DIRECTION AND COUNSELING

Spiritual life is original life. "Why," you may ask, "should there be another person to direct me in the unfolding of my original self? Why not simply seek out a kind of counseling that is non-directive?"

Non-directive counseling means I do not impose my ideas on the person who comes to me for guidance. I let him tell me what he himself feels like. I help him to clarify his problems instead of giving him my solutions.

Spiritual directors can benefit from insights gained by counselors. Attitudes fostered in counseling may prove advantageous in spiritual direction, provided the director harmonizes such attitudes with the unique purpose of spiritual guidance.

People should be listened to, also in spiritual matters. The Spirit of the Lord inspires each person to follow His teachings in his own way. A spiritual guide should help a man to find out what the Spirit wants of him. Non-directive counseling can teach the spiritual director something about the art of listening to what a person is really trying to say. But this is not the whole story.

The rest of the story is many thousands of years old. People of diverse cultures and religions—before and after our Lord—have tried to live the life of the Spirit. Sooner or later they ran into difficulties.

One of the lasting results of the original fall of man is a certain blindness in the realm of the spirit. We are inflicted with an inclination to greed and self-centeredness, with a hidden sensuousness, with a secret need to be something special in our own eyes and in the eyes of others. We crave excitement. We flee from daily life in fantasy. We have an almost invincible bent toward illusion and deception. We imagine we hear the voice of the Spirit when it turns out to be the voice of imagination, pride, passion. This self-deception can take the form of hysteria, hallucination, illusion, compulsion, fanaticism, and the paranoid pride of self-righteousness.

Once deception goes that far, it is difficult to help its victims. Convinced that the Spirit is speaking to them, they cannot listen to anyone else, whether he is a spiritual director, psychiatrist, psychologist, or physician.

The experience of mankind in regard to the dire consequences of self-deceptive spirituality led to the development of the function of spiritual direction. We find this institution in most religious cultures before Christ. It continued after Christ. The spiritual master, graced, experienced, and well-prepared, has a knowledge, a charisma, that enables him to assist others in finding the way. He is an enlightened authority in an area still closed to the experience of the person directed by him. Therefore, he cannot be merely non-directive.

As an example of non-directive counseling, take the case of a woman who has difficulties with her husband. The woman knows what good relationships with people should be like. Nobody has to tell her that. She can also come to know what her real feelings about her husband are. A non-directive counselor helps her to become aware of her feelings. She works them through with him. She finds out how she should change.

"Why," you may ask again, "can't the same thing be done in spiritual direction?"

The two situations are simply not the same. The case of the woman involves difficulties in everyday relationships. Everyone knows about such problems by the mere fact of living in his culture. It is not necessary to give the woman information about what an average relationship with a husband should be like. She knows that at least implicitly. She has to clarify her own feelings in relation to her husband. She has to sort out hidden resentments, hang-ups, defenses. The counseling relationship can help her to clarify what she knew only vaguely. It helps her to bring to light what she refused to know explicitly.

Men and women who want to live a spiritual life are in a different predicament. They want to venture out into a territory unknown in the everyday life of the individual: the realm of the spirit. Not having been there, they cannot know the pitfalls, the occasions for self-deception, the hidden attitudes that inhibit growth. A guide is needed. He must listen to their thoughts and feelings. He must take those psychological dynamics into account, but he has to do more than this. He must also speak to them with authority and experience about the ways of the spiritual life that are as yet unknown to them.

A spiritual director learns to distrust his personal prejudices and those of his culture. On the other hand, he knows and trusts the spiritual masters of his Church. He respects the uniqueness of each person. He is in tune with the age-old tradition of spirituality. He does not betray its universal wisdom. In its light, he tries to help each person understand what the Holy Spirit asks of him.

Lately, many people have become interested in the spiritual life. The only guides available to them may be counselors or people specialized in sensitivity training.

Since the seventeenth-century, there has been a decline of interest in spirituality. Traditionally, spiritual directors for the people came mostly from religious communities. This has been as true for the Catholic religion as for Far Eastern, Greek Orthodox, and Russian spiritualities. The reason was that the original religious communities were above all concerned to imbue their own members with the life of the Spirit. They did everything in their power to foster in their midst the development of outstanding and creative spiritual masters.

The spiritual wisdom of these communities resided in their great teachers and directors. These men and women, saintly, learned, and experienced in the ways of the Spirit, would initiate and direct the members of their communities in the spiritual life. They would teach and guide them with infinite tact and patience, pointing out pitfalls and dangers. The religious initiated by them would then go out among the people. Because of their own prolonged initiation by one of the outstanding masters of their community, many of them would be able in turn to initiate people outside their community in the spiritual life.

Later in the history of religious life in the West, religious communities stressed less and less the original concern to develop outstanding spiritual masters. New religious communities arose at the beginning of the industrial age. They were influenced by the organization of emerging armies, firms, and factories. Like the early companies, they went in for one practical purpose, such as *only* missions, *only* nursing, *only* teaching. Later on, industry specialized even more to insure higher production. Religious congregations followed a similar route. They became, for example, mission-oriented only for this type of territory or that kind of people, nursing only in old folk's homes, or teaching only for children of the rich or children of the poor. Such enterprises, their organization and staffing, tended to become a more central concern than the interest in spirituality.

Of course, religious communities before the industrial age were also involved in specific works. Often they were founded by secular priests or laymen already engaged in some kind of apostolic enterprise. This work became the occasion for their discovery of a need for a deeper spiritual life. Later they wanted the protection and inspiration of that spiritual life by the life of the vows. Therefore, they formed a religious community. The original occasion—the work they happened to do together—remained, however, an *occasion*. It never became the essence of religious life.

The essential meaning of religious life was to foster the personal and spiritual growth of each member. A member's effective engagement in some cultural work was one possible fruit of that spirituality. His specific work did not become the unchangeable essence of religious life as such. While the religious would usually be engaged by some of the works already developed by his order, spirituality came first.

This primary concern led to the preparation of masters of spirituality. As explained above, in this way spiritual masters became available not only for the community itself; people outside religious life also profited from their inspiration.

God's ways are not our own. In His own good time, He will restore the spiritual life as a central concern of Christianity. There are signs. For example, the Protestant monastery of Taizé has a remarkable rule. They do not begin with a rigid formulation of a practical aim—one highly specialized work, such as only foreign missions, only teaching, only nursing. The rule of Taizé speaks first of all of the personal and spiritual growth of each brother. All rules of life are oriented toward this primary meaning of religious life—not toward one or the other work in which the community may happen to engage itself during some cultural period.

If this trend continues, the concern for the life of the spirit may again prevail in Christianity. Such a new primacy of the spiritual life demands a new availability of spiritual masters. They should be both directive and non-directive. Non-directive insofar as they can listen to the originality of each person. Directive insofar as they must be courageous enough to discourage with authority any person who wants to go the wrong way because of motives for gain and status or because he wants to attain soothing feelings that *per se* have nothing to do with original spiritual values.

# X

## ENVY AND THE WORLD OF THE CHRISTIAN

Envy of
originality is one of the characteristics of the world
that Christ condemns. He says that His Kingdom is
not of this world. He tells me that I should be in the
world but not of the world. What does He mean by
"the world"?

He cannot mean the world or the cosmos that is
God's creation. What God created is good. He loves
this world. Christ condemns not creation as such but
what people made of creation.

Think about the word "world." "World" implies the
way I see the world. My world is what the world means
to me. In this sense I may read about the world of the
Indian, the world of the child, the world of the artist.
All these expressions say that my world is more for me
than a bland collection of people, things, events, and
natural resources.

The world in the human sense is never neutral. The
attitude of the Indian, the child, the artist makes for
the special meaning of their worlds. My world like
theirs is what I make of it. And what I make of it

depends on my way of looking at what is given in creation.

Christ condemns the world. He warns against the spirit of this world. He contrasts this world with His world, His Kingdom. What kind of outlook makes for the kind of world he condemns?

It must be a most fundamental outlook to which all people are inclined. He speaks about this condemned world in such a way that He does not limit it to one type of society, to some cultural period, to some race of people.

The world Christ warns against is a universal world of all times and all civilizations. This world is created and recreated by a universal human outlook—an outlook that has plagued man since time immemorial. The origin of this outlook is explained in the story of the fall of man. Man falls because he thinks he can save himself.

The myth that man can save himself takes different forms in different ages. The original sin of self-centeredness expresses itself differently in the Renaissance than in our times. Men of the Renaissance believed that a revival of art, literature, and aesthetics would bring salvation to mankind. Humanists today may believe as foolishly that science, socialization, or the ending of all wars will bring salvation. Such plans are commendable. But none of them—in isolation from God—can ever bring peace and salvation. What characterizes the spirit of this world is not so much these plans in themselves, but the arrogance of believing that mere human projects can bring salvation in an ultimate sense.

## The World Isolated from Christ

Adopting this spirit of the world, I isolate my world from Christ. I also isolate myself from man. If I see the world isolated from Christ, I cannot see in and behind my fellow men the mystery of Providence. This latter kind of seeing implies respect. Respect comes from the Latin *respicere* which means to look again. Respect is a way of looking again and again to discover original value in the other. The Christian is one who looks again and again in this deeper way. He is not only ready to discover the original value of a person behind his sins and deficiencies. He is also ready to discover the Value behind all values.

My respectful look discovers values in the other. It sees also the mystery of the Divine Will behind these values. In the light of faith, I accept without envy that values are given in different measure to different people. I wholeheartedly praise God for this.

Envy of original values in others is a typical characteristic of the world condemned by Christ. This is a world isolated from His Love and Grace. It becomes easily a field of envious competition. One reason for envious competition is the way I may feel about success and failure in case I cannot believe that Divine Love and Grace allows all things in this world to happen to me and everyone for the best.

I may then see personal success and failure as the

only factors that make life liveable. I easily envy the success of others that could have been mine were it not for an unreasonable piece of bad luck.

Loss of a living faith can stimulate envious competition also because of the absence of any belief in eternal values that transcend the value of a successful life in the competitive society. I may feel that after death all is finished for me. I do not believe in any divine consolation. Nothing can have its source outside of this self-sufficient world. The only meaning of life is to make this world a good place for all men and first of all for myself.

Success, status, and possessions cannot belong equally to all. But because the things I compete for have become ultimate values for me, I may feel envious if others have better luck than I in the acquisition of things. I may feel especially envious when I become aware that the source of their success is a certain originality I lack. What I envy then is their originality.

## Christian Respect

Christians are people who strive to conquer envy by respect, not merely human respect but divine respect. In the Spirit of Christ, I am open to all manifestations of the goodness of the Father in others. To live in the Spirit of Christ is to be sensitive to the original gifts granted to each man. This respect is divine because it is inspired by the Divine Spirit; it is an expression of the divine life of Christ in us.

ON BEING YOURSELF

Divine respect is possible only by divine grace; it recognizes divine gifts in others. This attitude leads to the Christian humanization of mankind.

Christ redeems me and my fellow men from our envy and value blindness. He does so in a radical and divine way. Even so, I will be contaminated again and again by the spirit of this world. I will fall back in envy repeatedly. But each time I do, Christ is waiting for me to return to His spirit. He restores my ability for true Christian humanization. Thanks to His Grace, I can look again with the respectful eyes of Christ. I can discover, admire, and affirm original values in my fellow men. The whole realm of values lights up for me. Present to Him, my world of values deepens and expands.

Respectful seeing of values stimulates me to foster the unique manifestations of such values in others. People when touched by this power of Christ are more open to human values. They are more ready to realize such values in this world. Divine respect is thus the radical overcoming of envy and the beginning of true humanization; such respect grants others their right to be original selves in service of God and man.

## XI

## ENVIOUS COMPARISON:
## OBSTACLE TO SPIRITUAL LIFE

Living in envy means that I am not centered in my true self. My life becomes one of comparison. I am forever asking what others have and what I am missing. When I find out that I have less than they do, I may try to diminish my sense of lack by belittling what is theirs.

As long as I live outside myself in envious observation of others, I cannot be myself. I can only begin to become myself when I accept what I am. I should not be preoccupied with the ways in which others differ from me. These differences tell me what I am not. I need to come to an awareness of who I am in relation to my Divine Origin.

God originates me continually. Were He to turn His face from me for a fraction of a second, I would no longer be. Each moment He makes me be in my uniqueness. He gives me my own hidden name which I will fully know only in eternity, a name nobody else has received or will receive.

## ON BEING YOURSELF

All things are created in and through the Word of God as so many little words. Each one of these words is unique. In and through the Divine Word, each person, thing, event is an unprecedented expression of the Divine. I too carry a unique message. My Father in heaven saw me from eternity in His Divine Word. He saw me as an original word in time and space. I should live up to my eternal originality. As a free person, however, I can deny my original design. For persons are different from things. Things cannot deviate from what they are created to be. I can. I can become a garbled word, a disgrace to *the* Word.

One way to become a mispronounced word is to live in envious comparison. Then I cannot hear what I am supposed to be. I am too busy comparing myself with others. Envy may diminish the effectiveness of God's unique expression in other persons too. Envious comparison may lead me to belittle others and gossip about them. I may sow the seeds of malicious suspicion about the intentions and actions of people whose original mission I unwittingly envy.

Why make fun of others who do things I secretly would like to do? Why not accept graciously my own modest place in the scheme of things? It is *my* place; it is as originally willed by God as theirs. Others may be called to be popular socializers, not I; great teachers or intrepid missionaries, not I; demonstrators or social activists whose names adorn the newspaper headlines, not I. I should not emulate or envy them. I must simply be myself as He wanted me to be from eternity.

I should see myself as emerging from His creative Will as originally as all other fellow "originals." I feel at-one with them in the Eternal Ground we share. They are as much a part of the divine orchestra as I. The player of the flute does not envy the player of the trombone because his sound is more majestic. He knows that the originality of each sound, in harmony with all others, constitutes the beauty of a symphony. The beauty of a symphony would be marred if one instrument would fail to play, or worse, try to imitate or outshine another.

God's symphony is a hidden symphony. Its ultimate and eternal beauty is known to the divine director, not to the players.

The history of salvation is a symphony rendered by countless players over the millennia with ever new instruments. The harmony of the symphony as a whole cannot be heard by the players of one short interlude. They cannot hear the grand performance that spans centuries and civilizations.

Not hearing the whole of God's symphony, I may be impressed by the sounds of some spectacular instruments. I may be inclined to call only those instruments original. I forget that their sound means nothing outside the harmony of the orchestra. To feel envious of so majestic a sound would be to forget to cultivate my own originality, the little sound I am called to be.

It is difficult to be faithful to the modest original word I am. What strengthens me is the Revelation that the Word of God became one of us. He lived in faithfulness to His original mission. His example enlightens me and radiates strength. It helps me to be my own limited word spoken by the Father. In and through Him, the incarnated Word, I can live as the original word I am by divine right and mission.

The Lord has placed me in this world to perform a task, to fulfill a mission in family, school, or company, organization, or neighborhood. But He can speak in me only when I am truly myself—not a replica of public opinion, not a thoughtless outgrowth of what the gang is saying.

*Envy, Task Dedication and Self-Motivation*

The Divine asks me to be faithful to my unique task in this world. I should perform this task with inspiration and conviction, with love and dedication. I should stand behind it as a responsible person.

The leveling of life may have robbed me of dedication. I have become part of the machine of modern life. One of the faceless public, I no longer know who I am.

To regain spiritual dedication to a task means to become a self-motivated person, not one who is blindly moved by others. Self-motivation does not mean that I necessarily do things differently. I share wholeheartedly many motivations which prevail in my culture. I try to make these motivations my own by letting them pass through my center. They become *self*-motivations.

Self-motivation cannot create a spiritual life in and by itself. Only grace can do that. But I can remove obstacles to the Holy Spirit. A most serious obstacle to His inspiration is absorption in the group. If I want to please others, to be one of the crowd, I may no longer stand behind my task as a self-motivated person. Doing a good job in a human and spiritual sense entails more than skillful performance. I should be personally involved in my work as I strive to embody my love for the Lord. This intention gives my performance, over and above skillfulness, a special quality. It links my work motivation with my deepest aspiration.

Because dedication is unusual today, it often evokes envy and irritation. It may be felt by others as a reproach. Inspiration arouses envy too. This envy is a threat to the work that God wants to accomplish within every person's unique situation.

A person may be aversely affected by the ridicule of envious leveling people. He may retreat not only in public but also in inner anonymity. While public anonymity may help a man to stay humble and inconspicuous, inner anonymity may lead to loss of personal dedication. Inner anonymity is my refusal to hear inwardly the unique eternal name God has given me.

I should learn to recognize how envious attacks by others can drive me into inner anonymity. Envy of others and their subsequent rejection and derision of my enterprises may tempt me to give up the personal centering of my life in the Divine. Loss of spiritual self-presence can lead to loss of personal dedication and diminished effectiveness in my task.

### Vigilance and Equanimity

The more naive I am about envy and its dynamics, the more I may evoke it. On the other hand, if I understand envy, I may learn the art of avoiding its arousal unnecessarily. I know better when to speak and to be silent, when to act and not to act, to care and not to care, to hide or step forward. I become a wise and watchful person on the alert for any word or move on my part that may unnecessarily evoke envy in my fellow men.

Does such vigilance make me tense? Is tenseness an obstacle to the life of the spirit? Does spiritual life not thrive better in equanimity?

It is not vigilance that makes me tense. It is the way in which I am vigilant. Vigilance can be willful, rigid, or violent, but it can as well be illumined by the spirit. Such vigilance is of the heart. It is modulated by a relaxed acceptance of limits in my life at this moment of my personal history. These limits tell me how vigilant I can reasonably be.

When I go beyond these limits, I feel it. I become tense, nervous, tired. These symptoms are signals that I must let go. I must relax my vigilance.

"Is it not possible," you ask, "that the envy of others will harm me when I no longer watch words or moves on my part that may arouse envy in them?"

Surely the danger is there, but you should not bother about it. You have done what you could within the limits of your *relaxed human* possibilities. What happens in spite of that, God allows to happen. You must take it in stride, suffer it for and with Him. Otherwise you will fail to meet another condition for the life of the spirit: that of equanimity, of not losing your rootedness in your center.

I must thus become aware of the strategies of envy of originality as they exist in and around me without losing equanimity. Gradually I may be able to be more present to the threat of envy in a relaxed way, but such spiritual maturing takes time and patience. Nonetheless, I need to see through myself and others in a loving and realistic way. Such perceptive caution helps me to respond more wisely to each situation. I should, however, maintain equanimity and abide in my center; otherwise my reaction to envy may become paranoid, immoderate, without tact and compassion, throwing me wide open to retaliation by others. The harmful things I may say when I have lost my centeredness are bound to catch up with me eventually.

In the beginning, it may be better to be less vigilant and to maintain my peace of mind. Gradually, then, I may grow in both equanimity and vigilance. The time may come when the gifts of the Holy Spirit elevate my vigilance to a higher plane—that of spontaneity—the mark of the person who has been spiritualized in the deepest reaches of his humanity. The gifts of the Holy Spirit illumine and strengthen the powers of man to such a degree that he has less difficulty in exercising the virtues asked by his situation. Virtue becomes more spontaneous, also the virtues of equanimity and vigilance.

## The Story of the Stone Cutter

The value of unenvious acceptance of my life and its simple rewards are charmingly portrayed in the Japanese tale of the stone cutter.

Once upon a time there was a stone cutter. Every day he went to the mountains to break stones out of rock. Out of the stones he fashioned doorsteps and grave stones. Being a good artisan he was always able to find buyers for his products. He never had to complain. To be sure, his income was modest and his work was heavy, but he was satisfied and did not desire anything else.

One day the stone cutter had to bring a tombstone to a rich man. It was an exhausting job. When he had arrived at the house of the rich man and looked inside he was surprised. The room was cool; the floor was covered with beautiful mats; a delicately painted print hung on the wall and under it stood a bouquet of fine flowers.

The stone cutter wiped the sweat from his brow and sighed: "Oh, if I were only a rich man, then I would not have to cut stone all day long."

To his astonishment he heard suddenly the voice of a good spirit, whom people believed to live in the mountains. The mountain spirit said to him, "Your wish will be fulfilled. You will be a rich man."

When the stone cutter returned that night to his hut with its thatched roof he could not believe his eyes. Where once had been his simple hut, there was now the house of a rich man. The floors were covered with beautiful mats; a splendidly painted print hung on the wall and under it stood a vase filled with beautiful flowers.

The stone cutter soon forgot his previous life. He enjoyed his riches.

One day, however, when the sun stood high in the sky and the weather was humid and oppressive, a retinue of noblemen passed his house. In the midst of them was the king. He sat in a palanquin carried by four footmen in red livery. A fifth footman held a golden parasol above the head of the sovereign and protected him against the rays of the sun.

Because it was very warm, the former stone cutter sighed: "Oh, if I were only a king. Then I too would be carried around in a palanquin and somebody would hold a golden parasol over my head."

No sooner had he said this when the voice of the mountain spirit rang out and cried: "Your wish will be granted. You will be a king."

And the former stone cutter became a king. Noblemen rode before and behind his palanquin carried by footmen in red livery; one footman held a golden parasol over his royal head protecting him against the rays of the sun.

But the summer was hot and the rays of the sun

came ever more strongly down to earth. The grass dried up, the brooks became empty, and, in spite of the protection of the golden parasol, even the face of the king became bronzed and heated.

When the king noticed what was happening, he thought: "What kind of ruler am I. The sun is more powerful than the king. If only I were the sun!"

The voice of the mountain spirit cried out: "Your wish will be fulfilled. You will be the sun."

And now he was the sun. Proudly he sent his rays to the earth. He scorched the grass and bronzed the faces of people, the faces of the poor and the faces of the rich, and also the faces of kings.

One day, however, a cloud appeared before the sun. And the sun exclaimed angrily: "Is a cloud more powerful than I? He holds my rays up and keeps them from going further. I want to be a cloud!"

The voice of the mountain spirit cried out: "Your wish will be fulfilled. You will be a cloud."

And now he was a cloud. He held the rays of the sun and shed his rain on earth; the rivers swelled and everywhere the waters rose. The dikes broke through and the dams collapsed; the waves dragged everything down. Only a high rock stood there unconcerned and looked down defiantly on the flood unchained by the rain.

When the cloud saw this he called out in astonishment: "What! A rock is more powerful than I! Then I want to be a rock."

No sooner had he said so when the mountain spirit

answered: "Your wish will be granted. You will be a rock."

And he became a rock. No flood, no matter how strong, could throw him off balance. He remained unmoved by the rages of the elements.

One day, however, he heard a strange noise. The rock looked down and saw a little human being, a stone cutter, who, with a pick axe, broke bits of stone out of his foot. The rock was overwhelmed by astonishment and exclaimed: "What? A miserable little man is stronger than the most powerful rock. Then I want to be a man!"

The voice of the mountain spirit sounded for the last time: "Your wish will be fulfilled."

And again he was the poor stone cutter of the past, earning his bread by the sweat of his brow. It was a scanty piece of bread—that was true. At times the sweat burned his eyes and he wound a cloth around his heated forehead, as is still the custom among stone cutters in Japan today. But in spite of his heavy task, he was happy. He had learned once and for all the wisdom that he who is not satisfied with himself, is satisfied with nothing.

## XII

## SPIRITUALITY AND COLLEGIALITY

My life extends itself in family, work, leisure, and social groups—all of which should be evaluated in light of the Spirit.

Many groups, such as social and charitable organizations, are trying to become collegial. If I am involved in these experiments, I must be guided here as in everything else by the Spirit of the Lord. I cannot know in advance precisely what He may ask of me in each new situation. If this were the case, I would no longer need His inspiration.

On Pentecost, the Spirit of the Lord spoke through His apostles in such a way that each one heard them speak in his own tongue. Pentecost is a reminder that the Spirit of the Lord is one of loving accommodation to each original person.

Collegiality enlightened by this Spirit can never mean the suppression of someone's personal calling by a vocal majority. The unique eternal call of each person—his own tongue—and what the Holy Spirit wants him to do, cannot be at odds with one another. Both came from God.

Collegiality, mellowed and illumined by the Spirit,

shows concern for what the call of each member of a social or charitable organization may be. It fears to impose on the person anything that could collide with God's Will for him. Such sensitivity demands detachment that only grace can give. A detachment from the plans of the organization when the Spirit clearly wants to use a member for something else. A detachment from envy when the individual thus called happens to obtain benefits unavailable to others. A detachment from my limited judgment when I realize that by background and education I am not capable of understanding why some member must do what he does the way he does it.

Collegiality of spiritual men who are humble and detached is a blessing. Collegiality without humility can be hell on earth.

Does that mean that each one can do what he wants, claiming the urge of the Spirit in him? By no means. I may misunderstand the communication of the Spirit. I may also mistake wishful thinking for divine inspiration.

The Spirit speaks mainly through the community— the community of the Church first of all. He may speak also through a collegial community or an organization of priests, religious, or laymen. Members of a collegial organization should liberate themselves from blind fascination with their own ideas. They should not be blinded by the prestigious plans of their organization. Then they may become a channel for the voice of the Spirit, who may speak in each person—priest, religious, or layman—who makes up a community, institute or organization. I should be cautious with what I experience as personal inspiration, willing to submit it to the judgment of others. I may also speak about it with a wise and trusted friend who knows me well.

It can never be the goal of collegiality to oblige everyone to divulge to all the members of the group the depths of his personal and spiritual life. Only few may live on the same wave length and sense what I am trying to say. The Spirit may use those who are naturally sensitive to the plight of a special type of person. He may enlighten and deepen the spontaneous under-standing they already possess. Collegiality in this case may mean that I find loving support also from those who are unable to understand me. They may be wise and humble enough to abide by the judgment of the few who may truly comprehend.

This seems to suggest that there are limits to collegial government. Collegiality may have value in regard to common external rules, provided these do not touch the intimate personality too deeply. The intimate personal dimension of life is not the ideal object of a collegial or team approach.

Abiding by the Spirit may mean at times that nobody can understand me. I must patiently wait until God in His good time enlightens those who can make it possible for me to follow the inner light.

For example, as a member of a Christian organization for peace, I may be deeply touched by the suffering war inflicts on people. I cannot bear it any longer. I want to set an example and to walk on foot to the capitol of my country in protest of war. The organization is run along collegial lines. No member is supposed to do such a special thing without dialogue with the other members who must consent to it if it is to be done in the name of the group.

They may turn my proposal down for many reasons. Maybe I have to postpone my project until they see that it is truly authentic for me. Maybe my project is not authentic after all. I must even be ready to admit that I may be deceiving myself. Everyone else can see it but not I. I may mistake excited daydreams and exalted ambitions for divine inspirations.

The suffering God then allows in me is twofold: the grief of not being able to accomplish what I feel is His Will for me; the pain of an illusion—as such unknown to me—which humiliates me in the eyes of others and disturbs me inwardly.

All suffering borne for His love, however, is purifying, also the tragic suffering of an illusion which I cannot overcome. In that case I should try to find a wise spiritual director or counselor who may help me to see what I cannot see as yet.

## XIII

## THREE SOURCES OF ORIGINALITY

God knows and cherishes me from eternity. He originates me in love. He brings me forth not the way cars are produced on an assembly line but with infinite care, with loving attention to the smallest and finest details. Eternal is His original project for me. When I become my self in Him, I come home to my eternal originality.

My eternal call manifests itself in time. It becomes visible in my life as lived in my body within a family, culture, and daily situation. This appearance of the eternal call in my daily life happens mainly in three ways.

### My Vital Self

What I am called to be is first of all revealed in my primordial body awareness. I could call this dimension of self the vital me. This vital awareness is influenced by the rhythm and intensity of the processes of my body, the various pulls and pressures of my glands and other organs, my particular metabolism, and the limits of my innate natural pace. An immediate result of this bodily constitution is my fundamental mood. This mood underlies my whole psychological outlook on myself and the world. From such agents emerge my temperament and temperamental disposition. This constellation of factors is as unique as my fingerprints; it is the highly individualized ground plan of my personality. This vital ground of my originality cannot be changed much as long as my bodily constitution stays the same. It is the innate blueprint of my style of life. It is the voice of God speaking in my body. My vital self, in interaction with my environment, is thus a first revelation of my eternal destiny.

## Family and Tradition

This first revelation is joined by a second one. I am born in a family. This family is not an isolated unit. My family is immersed in a Catholic community. In and through my family, I belong to the Catholic people. To belong to this people means to share in a certain spirit or spirituality. This spirit affects my family's thoughts, feelings, dreams, and fantasies, their plans and projects, their words, behavior and customs. In and through all of these characteristics the spirituality of my family affects me.

Already in the womb of my mother, I may have been affected by her traditional ways of doing things and taking care of herself. After birth, the influence of my family on me is undeniable. In countless ways, by stories and symbols, by words and customs, I become immersed in a Catholic spiritual tradition. This happens long before I can consciously take this tradition up and make its essence my own.

This early influence is so much a part of me that I can never shut it off totally. Childhood tradition will remain with me as an invitation, a challenge, an inclination, a reproach, an indestructable memory. I can fight it; I can deny it; I can turn to other traditions; I can attempt to assimilate a whole new type of spirituality. But I must integrate the new way with the essence of my familial spirituality. Otherwise I will be alienated from the second source of my originality. I lose touch with the tradition in which I am immersed from the beginning of my life. I lose touch with a part of myself.

God allows me to be born in this tradition. Family tradition is the second revelation of His unique plan for me. This second source of my originality is not isolated in its effects from that of my vital self. What comes forth from both sources unites, as it were, into one stream. From the beginning, I take up the spiritual tradition of my family in a unique way. My vital self, which spontaneously imbibes this living tradition, is unique. The ways of the family become really a living part of me in this prepersonal phase of my life. Often I cannot distinguish any longer between my vital self and those spiritual orientations

*Three Sources of Originality*

I spontaneously absorbed at home as a Western Catholic child.

In childhood this spirituality is not yet mine in the personal sense. It is merely a prepersonal vital-familial self-orientation. It will incline me to feel, think, and act in certain directions. Later I will be awakened to the personal life of the spirit. Then it will be necessary to separate the kernel of this tradition from its incidental accretions.

The spiritual dimension of my self can never be isolated from the vital dimension. My integral self is an integration of all self-dimensions. The ground dimension of my self, the vital me, speaks therefore in my most spiritual endeavors, in my deepest intimacy with God in Christ. In this sense I can see a unity between the project of my uniqueness as written by God in my body and the project of my uniqueness as revealed in my historical immersion in a spiritual tradition.

*Personal Spiritual Life*

A third revelation of God's plan for me is experienced in my personal spiritual life as lived in my daily situation. This is the actual ongoing revelation of God's call for me. His revelation in daily life invites me to take up and integrate personally and critically the first and second revelations. I must do that in light of my life situation in which the Spirit speaks.

I should be open to all three revelations steadily

deepening my understanding of each one of them. Then I will be able to harmonize them. The more I approximate this harmony, the more I will become faithful to my divine originality. When I close myself off from one of these sources of my original and eternal destiny, I become split, alienated, and at odds with myself.

## Dialogue Between These Dimensions

In different periods of my life, I may be tempted to close myself off from one or the other of these three intimations of God's call for me. I may forget to listen to the first voice of God, that which speaks in my situated vital self. For instance, I may become fascinated by public projects that happen to be in at the moment. I stop listening to my own vital needs and possibilities as they have developed in interaction with my childhood environment. I go against the basic structure of my personality. I do not hear the warning voice of God in the complaints of my body. I do not unfold my own possibilities for a spiritual life. I follow blindly some kind of popular religious mood or project which may be at odds with the unique vital person I am.

Another temptation is to close myself off from the second source of divine intimation, namely, the essential core of my spiritual tradition. I discover other traditions rooted in other religions or in humanistic religious movements. I become aware of the limitations of my own religious heritage. I feel a new enthusiasm for universal, limitlessly open, general attitudes. They seem to embrace all possible religious and human truth.

The possibilities suggested by these attitudes are a fiction of the imagination. Limitless and structureless openness to all truth is inhuman: first of all because man can only know from a limited historical perspective; and secondly because to strive after this impossible openness to everything robs me of my innermost possibility—to become the unique human being I am called to be within the horizon of my limited situated tradition.

I can only find my full identity by entering as deeply as I can into the essence of my Catholic spiritual tradition. I absorbed this source of originality in my family. I have to deepen it by immersing myself in the spiritual life of the Church. I have to participate in its prayer as it comes to me in the liturgy.

Within the limits of my possibilities and state of life, I should try also to nourish myself with the wisdom of the saints. And I should read in a meditative way spiritual writers who are recognized by the Catholic community as having lived the essence of Catholic spiritual tradition.

This homecoming to the second source of my divine uniqueness may be necessary at times. I may have been over-involved in ecumenical, humanistic or secular endeavors. I may have lost contact with my own roots. Perhaps I have lost myself in attempts to integrate non-Christian traditions into the Catholic one. In this case, too, I may have neglected to dwell in my own spiritual tradition. As a result I feel self-alienated. A homecoming becomes necessary.

Finally, I may be well aware of the demands of my vital self and of the richness of my Catholic spiritual tradition, but be deaf to the voice of the Holy Spirit in my daily life where He reveals to me the Will of God. He speaks to me uniquely in the spiritual dimension of my self. This spiritual dimension of my self unfolds in dialogue with my daily life situation.

Deafness to the unique intimations of the Divine Spirit may be a result of immoderate involvement in causes and ideals. I may be lacking in stillness and recollection. The voice of God heard in my vital self and in my original tradition must be complemented by my listening to the voice of God in my innermost self or spirit. My innermost self is, in turn, illumined by my life situation. Without this situated listening, it would be impossible for me to understand what God intends for me personally here and now. This listening clarifies for me His messages in my vital self and in the tradition communicated to me from infancy on.

On the other hand, I would be mistaken to make my *present* life situation the *only* source of my originality. In listening to my present life situation, I must be aware of dangers. I can easily deceive myself. I may mistake the voice of my egoism, of my self-fascination, of my elated idealism for the voice of the Spirit in my life situation. I may then do foolish things, which would be at odds with my vital possibilities and limitations. Such acts may also overlook the essence of my original tradition as appropriated within the Catholic community. Should this happen, I again become self-alienated. A harmonious spiritual life, faithful to the fullness of my originality, becomes impossible.

To make my vital self the *only* source of my original life would be a mistake too. Temperamental inclinations rooted in my vital make-up should be taken into account. They are an outline of my possibilities and limitations. However, they tell me far more what I should *not* do than what I should do. To know the temperamental form of my acts is one thing. But to know the positive content of my personal acts, I need something else. I need the other two sources of my originality: the voice of the Catholic community and the inspiration of the Holy Spirit in my present life situation.

When I listen only to the voice of the Catholic community, I may lose my way too. This voice tells me the general way I should be in the world as a Catholic Christian. However, there are many ways open for me to live this common Christian style of life. I have to choose which of these ways is most faithful to my personal calling. Then I have to make this way uniquely my own. I must take into account the message of my vital self and of my spiritual self in dialogue with my daily situation.

There should thus be a constant dialogue between the situated vital, traditional, and spiritual dimensions of my self. Only in this dialogue can my true self emerge into the fullness of an original harmonious spiritual life.

# XIV

## SPIRITUAL LIFE AND VITAL ORIGINALITY

The potential original style of my spiritual life is first of all revealed by God in the vital me. When I go against God's will as expressed in my vital self, I may feel symptoms of disturbance. They warn me that I have lost God's path for me.

For example, I may read about a person who grows spiritually by the expression of his prayerful presence to God in social labor among the most poor under revolting conditions. His example inflames my imagination. I find myself in an exalted frame of mind; I would like to do the marvelous things he is doing. I become even more enthusiastic when his apostolate is hailed as *the* expression of religion in our time. I forget that the cultural expression of spirituality is manifold; it can never be identified with one type of cultural activity.

The essence of spirituality is graced originality. The Grace of God gently takes up what is most personal in me. Spiritual life is inspired by the unique invitation God extends to me in tune with the way in

*Spiritual Life and Vital Originality*

which He allows me to develop genetically, personally, and spiritually. God calls certain individuals to live their spiritual life and its cultural expression in a similar way. They may form together an action group or organization or a new cultural movement. I am not necessarily called to share such a cultural expression of the spirituality of others, even if they are a majority. I must first of all listen to the revelations of God's Will in the vital me.

The apostolic or social elations of others should not determine my way of life. Neither should I try to brainwash others to engage themselves in the kind of apostolate or social action that happens to be the way in which my unique spirituality spontaneously embodies itself. In that case, I would try to play God for others.

## Listening to My Vital Self

Listening to the reactions of my vital self helps me to become aware of unfaithfulness to God's plan. How do I bodily react to a social involvement that some may praise as *the only* way to God? Can I stand up under a task which seems to agree so well with some of my friends? Do I become tense and unhappy? Not only in the beginning but continuously?

Not everyone receives from God a body predisposed for this kind of life. I must admit that God may tell me through my body that I should express my spirituality differently.

For example, I may become impressed by the musical way in which some people express their presence to God and man. I would like to do the same. I try to sing, to play an instrument. I have no ear for tone and melody, no feel for rhythm, no dexterity with stringed instruments. These limitations of my emotionality, brain, body, and senses tell me that this is not the way God is asking me to express my spiritual call.

Or I may be affected by the "encounter fever." Some of my friends or colleagues feel best in personal encounters with people to whom they want to bring Christ. I myself may not be blessed with a sensitive temperament. By nature I am more the cool, reserved, intellectual type. This means that God wants me to grow in a different direction than my excitable and sensitive colleagues. They would be foolish to demand that my love for Christ should be expressed in the same way as theirs. I may give in to this demand, but it would mean a betrayal of the Will of God for me. For I am not at ease with this kind of self-expression, no matter how hard I try to be.

*Humble or Arrogant Enthusiasm*

Never do anything because others are doing it or because it is the thing to do nowadays.

A person may rave to others about his teaching, administration, mission work, efforts for peace or racial justice, art, writing, or manual labor. Without consciously intending it, he may seduce others to do his thing instead of their own. In his enthusiasm, he lures them away from God's Will for them.

Be on the lookout for how a person expresses his enthusiasm. Is his a humble or an arrogant zeal?

Arrogant zeal contains hidden scorn. It pities those poor creatures who are not generous enough to take part in the great missionary, ecumenical, theological, or social effort of our times.

The haughty religious enthusiast is not afraid that he may detract you from your own mission. He does not live in fear and trembling that he may take you away from God who speaks in your uniqueness. He may confuse you by subtly evoking guilt feelings in you. He makes you feel bad for not doing his thing. He tries to lure you away from your own divine task. He paints vivid pictures of the holiness of the work he himself is doing. The religious fanatic at his worst may even engage in political maneuvers. He may try to get religious organizations to encourage blindly all members to engage themselves in the apostolic, missionary, or social tasks in which he happens to be engaged.

Humble zeal is different. Its foundation is gratitude. God allowed me to find my special task in life. I may live now by His Will as expressed in my unique make-up and fundamental disposition. Never should I disparage others who do not have the same disposition, who can not feel at home in my enterprise. Surely, I may show how beautiful this task can be for those who are really called for it. I want to make known that such a task exists for those who feel disposed that way.

Humble zeal never suggests that anyone not so disposed should feel compelled to undertake a certain task. This person is too humble to play God. He leaves it up to God alone how many people He disposes in His own good time for a social or missionary venture.

A modest apostolic worker never elevates his own engagement as *the* engagement for all *really* generous people. Neither does he imagine that he alone makes sacrifices. He realizes that each person should work for the Kingdom of God. He should do so in accordance with his vital possibilities and limitations. He knows that man experiences a fundamental security and at-homeness when he can do something that is not at odds with his personal make-up. But he realizes also that each man will encounter sooner or later sacrifices in the kind of work he is doing, even if this work agrees with his personality.

A Christian may be engaged in social and political action. He is usually a person who is at-home in such actions. This does not exclude, however, that he will encounter suffering within this activity. His at-homeness in this work, however, is one of the elements that will carry him through. Others might be destroyed psychologically, spiritually, physically.

The same man of social action may feel that it would be impossible for him to spend his working years behind a desk or in a laboratory like the Christian scholar or scientist. He should not forget that a Christian scholar is not merely blessed with good intelligence as numerous others; more importantly, he has a specific temperament rooted in his vital make-up that conditions him to feel at home with classrooms, books, statistics, and laboratory tools. Within this compatible expression of his spirituality, however, he too will meet his own suffering: hours of boredom, intellectual frustration, misunderstanding by students and colleagues, mental exhaustion. Here again his vital at-homeness will carry him through such adversities. Lack of the same at-homeness could destroy a man of missionary or social action, who would be forced to play the professor or scholar at some university.

## Problem of One-Sided Enthusiasm

If I do not take into account my vital predisposition, I am bound to harm my self-unfolding before God. I may also lessen the effectiveness of the works in which I have enlisted myself. Arrogant zeal can become epidemic. It can do damage to the Church and the world. Epidemic enthusiasm can suddenly emerge. People in the Church discover a need that has been neglected. It has been disregarded usually because of a past enthusiastic zeal to meet other needs. These needs, in turn, were the result of a former neglect, and so on.

For example, in a certain period of the culture, the life of the spirit may not have been expressed sufficiently in higher realms of education. Alarmists cry out in holy indignation. Numerous colleges and universities are established. All kinds of Christians—religious and non-religious—are exhorted to express their spiritual life in academic positions. The result can be disastrous. Men and women, not really at-home in this milieu, may be presssured into a scholarly life. Because they are not at-home in academic work, they will engage "on the side" in other apostolic enterprises, instead of spending the time with their books and becoming first-rate scholars of a Christian inspiration.

As a result of this one-sided periodical interest in academic needs, other needs may be neglected. Suddenly there is an outcry for apostolic and missionary workers. Touched by the common hysteria, numerous people may now rush blindly into that field with the same deplorable consequences. Many who do not belong there and who would be better off in academic life may lead unhappy and ineffective lives in the wrong places.

To give another example: in a certain period of our culture, it may be discovered that the children of political, industrial, and economic leaders are not sufficiently touched by the Spirit of God. Again a nervous excitement arises to fill this need at once. Both religious and laymen try to close the gap by organizing educational programs for these children. Without knowing it, they may be laying the ground for the next emergency. Now the poor are neglected. When this is discovered, a new one-sided enthusiasm takes hold of the community of believers. Everyone rushes to take care of the poor. They neglect the Christian inspiration of those who are well established cultural and economic leaders.

Can we ever get out of this vicious circle? Has religious hysteria to repeat itself century after century? One way out may be to respect deeply the Will of God as it speaks in the unique vital self of each person. In that case, we may find the right people for the right work. Respectful presence to the individual calling of each Christian may help us to overcome our hysterical overreaction to a momentary emergency. It may help us to break out of the vicious circle of neglecting one dimension of the Kingdom when we panic about another. Such an outlook, however, presupposes that we primarily concentrate on the style and nature of each man's unique spiritual life and only secondarily on the countless different works in which this spiritual life may express itself.

## XV

## SPIRITUAL LIFE AND FAMILIAL ORIGINALITY

I am what I am partly because of my family. To be sure, the first source of what I am is my vital self. For I am rooted in my biological make-up and in the fundamental mood and temperament that flows from it.

The vital me, however, is faced from the beginning with the family in which I am born. Before I am able to think things over personally, I have to adapt myself to the people who take care of me, a defenseless infant. My family affects the way I will live out my vital originality. This first influence, good or bad, will leave its mark on me for life.

The spiritual dimension of my personality cannot be isolated from the vital or familial dimension of the same unique self that I am. The mystery of the Divine Will speaks not only in my body but also in the history of my growth within the family. If my family was loving and tender, their care may have enhanced my dispositions for kindness and love. By the same token, this disposition may make me more vulnerable later in life when I meet harsh or painful situations.

*Spiritual Life and Familial Originality*

Perhaps my family was severe, strict, and reserved in its expressions of affection. In that case, I may become distant, cool, and somewhat withdrawn, especially if these attitudes tie in with my vital originality. Such an early orientation in the family at least predisposes me for a spirituality more cool, less expressive. I probably prefer to express this spirituality in practical and intellectual pursuits that allow me to keep a certain distance from people.

## Family Influences Spiritual Life Style

The influence of vital and familial originality is so strong that even the finest spiritual men manifest an amazing range and variety of life styles. Take the quiet absent-minded style of St. Thomas Aquinas. Once St. Thomas went to an exclusive dinner offered by the king. The king and his guests were engaged in good-natured conversation, in praise of the delicious food and sparkling wine. St. Thomas sat still in quiet contemplation. Suddenly, in forgetfulness of time and place, he banged the table with his fist and cried out, "I have found it, the argument against the Albigenses." There was a hushed silence around the table. The guests looked anxiously at the king. What would he say about such a break in court decorum?

Fortunately for St. Thomas the king was a broad-minded man. He did not give him a lecture on decorum; instead he ordered a servant to bring in writing material so that the saint could write down the argument that he had found while immersed in contemplation at the king's table. The king by this gesture proved his own greatness—a greatness of mind that can respect any style of life that God gives to man.

That a saintly man is called by God to such intellectual heights that he forgets even the king and the royal guests at an exclusive banquet is an extreme example. However, it serves to illustrate that such a man as St. Thomas can do little about what he fundamentally is. He has to accept the bliss and the pain of his uniqueness as an expression of God's Will.

Spiritual life is not possible as long as a person rejects God's Will for his life. As long as he refuses to accept his destiny, he is fighting God. He may do so because well meaning friends, family members, or superiors may suggest to him that to be holy he should be what he is not. Suggestions seducing the person away from the Divine Will may have come from unenlightened spiritual directors. The danger is compounded by family and peer group as well. Under the threat of banishment, the peer group may impose their codes indiscriminately on everyone. Only the strong can resist. Even then they may need a special grace to withstand the seduction of peer groups when their originality obliges them to do so.

St. Thomas would have been wrong to try anxiously to become an expert socializer. God had not made him this way. Regardless of what peers or colleagues thought, he had to be true to himself.

A totally different type was St. Philip Neri. He expressed his spirituality by enriching life not through the solitary writing of a *Summa Theologica* but by humorous comments and practical jokes that made life more pleasant for all who encountered him. It would have been against his nature to be as quiet, absent-minded, and contemplative as St. Thomas.

Or take the difference between St. Francis de Sales and St. Francis of Assisi. During his whole life, St. Francis de Sales remained a refined and cultured nobleman who expressed and lived his spirituality in exquisite language, in cultured surroundings, and in gentle moderation. The Poor Man of Assisi left the home of his merchant father to embrace Lady Poverty and live in harsh surroundings, adorned only by the beauty of nature.

What about the difference between St. Ignatius of Loyola and St. John Bosco? The first was a highly disciplined, intellectual administrator, and an ascetical preacher of the *Spiritual Exercises.* For a lifetime, he was influenced by the virtues of a good soldier as taught in his knightly family. The latter was a warm outgoing lover of street urchins, radiating on a spiritual level the earthly warmth of his Italian peasant family.

We can go on and on. The examples are countless. From them we learn one main thing: never to fight what we fundamentally are. What I am is written in my body and in my history within my family. My spiritual life has to be a life of union with the Will of God, as expressed in my family and early history. To unite God's Will I have to unite myself with the expression of that Will in my vital and familial self.

## ON BEING YOURSELF

### Family History and Spiritual Originality

What does it mean to accept God's Will as expressed in my history within the family? Does it mean that I must think, feel, and act exactly as my family did? Must I be a carbon copy of my parents? Not at all. Just compare the lives of the children that come from the same family. They are usually very different. This is because the family can only exercise its influence on children who are already endowed with a vital make-up. This vital make-up is different in different children; hence the way the family affects each child is different too.

Moreover, the family itself is different for each child. Except in the case of twins, the children are born at different times and thus the family is in a different stage of development. It has undergone new experiences which alter, however slightly, its outlook, ambitions, values, and intimate relationships. Each newcomer to the family also has to take into account the presence of former children, who have already developed a special relationship with their parents and with each other. So each child is in some sense faced with a different family even if in the same family.

As the child grows up, he gains insight and freedom. He becomes aware of the family influence upon his life and begins to take a free stand toward his past. He may accept or reject the standards of his family. So too, when the child awakens to the spiritual dimension of his personality, he begins spontaneously to evaluate the influence of his family in the light of his presence to the

Sacred. Again he is led to a selective acceptance or rejection of family values and influences.

## Positive and Negative Family Influences

If rejection of family values is possible, how can we maintain that the familial self has a lasting influence on our spiritual originality? Let us emphasize again that the family influence does not necessarily determine that we will foster this or that idea, attitude, or custom in our lives. As a matter of fact, spiritual originality may imply that we give up many of the opinions, perceptions, and habits we valued as children. These acquired norms may prove to be at odds with the basic structures of our vital self; or they may be in conflict with the revelation of God's Will in our life situation.

In what sense, then, can we say that our family history plays a lasting role? In a most basic sense. Our spiritual personality would be fundamentally different if we had been born and raised in another family. My family in this country, in this town, provides me with a storehouse of experiences that leave traces on my life that can never be washed away totally. This store of experiences is, as it were, the primary capital with which I have to work. It can be compared to the stone or wood in which a sculptor has to inscribe his original creation. He can do all kinds of things with the marble, but no matter what he does he is dependent on the slab and limited by it. The same is true of the experiential material offered me by my family.

No matter how fully I develop in my spiritual life, I

have to take into account my family experiences. I can re-evaluate them in all kinds of ways; I can flow with them or react against them. The only thing I cannot do is ignore their ever present reality. The more a sculptor becomes aware of all the possibilities and limitations of his material, the more free he becomes to work with it. Similarly the more I become aware of the experiences in my family and their hidden impact on me, the more I will be able to take them up into my spiritual life and make the best of them.

With God's Grace, I may be able to diminish the negative influences of certain family attitudes. I may purify and spiritualize the good experiences at home and the power they continue to exert on my personality. This effort entails a process of self-discovery that can be painful. There is the danger that I may become angry temporarily with my father or mother, brothers or sisters. Such hostility can make me bitter and resentful. Bitterness and resentment prevent the equanimity which is a condition for spiritual harmony. For this reason, the discovery of myself as the product of a family which influenced my subsequent orientation should be accompanied by the work of forgiveness.

I must become aware of any resentment I may rightly or wrongly harbor towards my parents, brothers, or sisters. Then I must try to forgive them. For they themselves could not be totally free in their opinions, feelings, and actions. They too were dependent on their parents, their teachers, their·

culture. They may not have been as graced as I by a spiritual awakening. I did not deserve this light. It was a gift that came to me from God.

Whenever resentment emerges, then, such considerations may gradually help me to overcome the last vestiges of bitterness in my heart. Working this way at the original material of experience given to me by my family, I may harmonize the familial with the vital and spiritual dimensions of my originality, while at the same time overcoming the hidden resentments that mar my equanimity.

## XVI

## UNION WITH THE DIVINE WILL IN DAILY LIFE

The vital, familial, and cultural dimensions of my self tell me more what I should not do than what I should do. They point to my destiny more in a negative than in a positive way.

Say. that I am a person with delicate constitution, a nervous temperament, often ill, easily tired—a person who needs quiet surroundings and plenty of rest. By family background, I am sensitive, shy, and withdrawn. Cultural influences, together with my vulnerable physical make-up and family background, have made me an intellectual type, a man of refined taste, aesthetic, speculative, somewhat impractical, and out of touch with the common run of man.

These dimensions of my self tell me that I should not become a prize fighter, a marine, a used car salesman, a bartender, or a baseball coach. Many more hobbies, jobs, and life styles, delightfully appropriate for others, are clearly out for me. If I listen to God's Will speaking in my temperament, disposition, and past history, I know what a disaster I would be as a longshoreman, professional wrestler, or lonely explorer of the North Pole.

My constituted self, however, cannot tell me in and by itself what I should do, what life style, hobbies, and work I should choose, or how God wants me to behave in certain situations. I need to evaluate personally and creatively my concrete life situation to know what is best for me in regard to central and decisive options in my life.

This evaluation should be done not only from my narrow perspective. I should ask myself what I, as this unique person, can best do from the viewpoint of the whole situation in which I find myself. How does God speak to me in this situation? What does he seem to be asking me as the unique person I am at this moment of my life? Being the person I am, does he ask me to serve humanity as a house painter, piano tuner, librarian, third grade teacher, artist, writer?

If I am trying to live a spiritual life, I will ask myself such questions in the light of His Holy Will. The vital, familial, and cultural dimensions of my self receive a more positive meaning when they are thus taken up in my spiritual life. In and through my spiritual life, they enter into dialogue with my daily life. This dialogue unfolds in the light of the Holy Spirit. Through it, I discover what God wants me to be so that I can grow to the stature of His call for me.

This dialogue is twofold. I am not only in dialogue with the present. I maintain some kind of dialogue with the past. This latter dialogue, however, is not central. It is, as it were, an "aside," a "taking into account" of my past.

Take, for example, the famous painter Pablo Picasso, living in France during World War II. Without judging the moral quality of his life or setting him up as an example to be followed in all respects, we can relate the story of one choice he made in the light of his past—a choice that might have been right for him if made out of the right motives.

He had always spoken out against persons who would trample on the rights of others. The invaders of France and the traitors of its people were doing just that. Would Picasso put his life on the line? Would his deeds be as strong as his words? Would he join the resistance like thousands of others? Was he just a big talker in his house and a coward in the street? Picasso did not join the resistance. He did not lift a finger to expel the invaders or immobilize the traitors or save the persecuted. Should we, therefore, brand him a phony? Not necessarily.

Picasso had to dialogue with the painful situation in which he found himself. He must have asked himself seriously how he, with his unique vital, familial, and cultural background, could respond best to this challenge of history. He decided that what he could do best was to retire to his atelier and paint tirelessly to create symbolic expressions of the horror of war and injustice. Picasso was honestly convinced that he should take into account his personal and cultural past while looking for his unique answer to the times. His dialogue ended with the conclusion that the best gift he could give to mankind was his paintings. To create them he needed quiet retirement not the noise of the battlefield. He felt he would be more effective for humanity as a painter than as an operator of machine guns and explosives. This decision would have been a religious one had it come about as a result of Picasso's prayerful listening to the Sacred in events such as these.

I too must keep an eye on the past when making up my mind about actions to be taken here and now. Dialogue with the Divine Will implies that I take into account what I already am. I keep in touch with God's Will speaking in my past. Central, however, is my dialogue with the Will of God in my present situation.

This dialogue is not only a discovery of what I already am but also a reaching out to what I may become. Dialogue with the "situated" Will of God is creative. Out of this meeting with His Holy Will emerges a new me. This new evolvement is not contained in my past like an oak in an acorn. I begin to become myself in ways I could not foresee. The spiritual me is thus not something to be found but to be created. As spirit, I am a reaching out to what I am not yet.

## Mystery of My Originality

God's Will appears everywhere. It is first of all in me, in everything I am and do. I must "catch" the Divine Will at work in myself. I must find it at the root of my thoughts, feelings, actions.

ON BEING YOURSELF

Each time I arrive at the originating source of action, emotion, reflection, I am faced with a unique manifestation of God's preserving and allowing will. I can rest in this Ground. I can quietly participate in the sustaining and originating Divine Will at the base of what I think, feel and do. I do not feel lonely there. I flow with the mysterious Power of the Divine.

## Divine Will in Daily Life

It is not enough, however, to meet the Divine Will in myself alone. My inner life is most near to me; however, my self in turn reaches out to all things in life that have meaning for me. In some sense, these outward meanings are an extension of my self. They form, as it were, my expanded self where I must find God's Presence too. My awareness of God's Will in everything inside and outside me unifies all my experiences. My self includes my whole world. Everywhere in that world is the Will of God. His Will is the origin of all things, the beginning and end, the Alpha and the Omega (Rev. 1:8).

The Divine Will underlies all people, things, and events. Presence to this Will in daily life restores the art of integrated living. I go beyond the limited field of my practical concerns. I become aware of my at-oneness with His Original Presence. Such deepened awareness helps me to distance myself from the agitations of my surface perception. Agitation causes me to overlook many sides of the situation with which I must deal. It makes me less effective. Moreover, surface agitation devours my energy if I do not keep it in check. If I allow my concerns to run wild, I only become more tired, irritable, and less effective. At-oneness with the Source of my life recharges my vital energy and renews my spirit.

## The Simple Way of Union

The way towards union with God's Will in dialogue with daily life must be simple. I may be blind to this way, not because He made it difficult, but because my vision is obscured by the sinfulness that came into the world with the fall of man.

Still there must be a simple way back. A way that demands no gross departure from the common ways. A way that does not diminish my effectiveness, but instead enhances my capacity to know, to achieve, to enjoy. A way that fills a void, a need felt by men everywhere. A simple way of communion with my Divine Origin as originating me and others and my life situation here and now.

This way is the path to the kingdom within that our Lord spoke about. A Christian, who has discovered this way and strives to live it, will radiate the peace of at-oneness with the Father. This peace fills the atmosphere around him and may communicate itself to those he meets. His is the peace of an integrated life, the wisdom of at-oneness with the Divine Will, which manifests itself in him and in all around him.

# ON BEING YOURSELF

## *Deepest Meaning of Self and Others*

My life, my self is not confined "within my skin." It is nourished by the people I meet, the things I do, the events I face. I am touched by these people, things, and events and I touch them in turn. My self stretches out as far as my experience. All that has meaning for me in some way is me.

Pretend I am a mailman. The drab office where I pick up my mail, the sunny, windy, rainy, or snowy streets I walk through day after day, the faces of the people I see at the same windows and doors, their spirited dogs who bark at me without fail—they all have become a part of my everyday life. They all live in and for me in a special way. They would not have the same lively meaning for a stranger who would walk for the first time through my village. I meet a variety of people every day while doing my job, some kind or hostile, others trusting or suspicious, cheerful or moody. At times I am faced with unpleasant events. Letters get lost. Packages are stolen. All these happenings have diverse meaning for me. But as a spiritual person, I can believe in an overall meaning, a meaning that unites all the meanings of these people, events, and things that make up my daily life. God allows them to be, to occur, to unfold.

If all of these things had only diverse meanings, they could not be integrated by me. They would tear me apart. That is why it is important to live the meaning in which I myself and they share. This deepest meaning is our common Origin. The Divine

Will speaks in me and in all of them. The more I become one with this Divine Will, flowing with it, the more will peace be mine. To be at one with God's Will, I must see its light in all things. Without this Will, nothing could be. This awareness is the root of a peaceful and effective life.

## Following Christ

The Divine Will is the deepest reality in heaven and on earth. Nothing can equal the ever-present power of God's Will. This Will rules all things under all circumstances.

My own life too emerges from the Will of God. I can refuse to go along with His Will. I can resist His plan over my life. If I do so, I forgo my best possibility for self-unfolding.

"Your will be done on earth as it is in heaven" (Mt. 6:10). In heaven the Divine Will finds no resistance. I must try not to resist this Will here on earth. My Father in heaven must be at the center of my life. "Doing the will of him who sent me and bringing his work to completion is my food" (John 4:34). These words reveal the attitude of my Lord. His whole life was steeped in the Will of the Father. His is the way for all men who want to be their true selves before God.

The life of the Christian is a life of at-oneness with Him. Following His way must be simple enough to be understood and practiced by all. That is why the following of Christ could be summed up as doing the

ON BEING YOURSELF

Will of the Father. "You will live in my love if you keep my commandments, even as I have kept my Father's commandments, and live in his love" (John 15:10).

To do as Christ did, I must live the Divine Will at each moment. Only one thing matters: to listen at every moment to the Will of the Father. This is the way for everyone to be himself as God wants him to be. No other way is given to man. "I am the way, and the truth, and the life; no one comes to the Father but through me" (John 14:6).

*Acceptance of My Original Calling in Christ*

My spiritual life is thus the life of Christ within me. I allow Him to take over my life as if it were His. Christ helps me to follow the Will of His Father for me. He helps me to listen to His Spirit. Instead of keeping closed to the Holy Spirit, I am asked to yield to His inspiration. Thus, to live the life of Christ is to be open as He was to the Will of the Father through the inspiration of the Holy Spirit.

The Spirit speaks in many ways. He may speak in a way that is out of the ordinary, though this is a most unusual event. It would be foolish to wait for such a thing to happen. I should not wait for an extraordinary message from the beyond, for, in the meantime I may remain deaf to the whisperings of the Spirit in everyday life.

Led by the Spirit of my Lord, I must look at the simple events of my daily life, its duties and demands.

demands. I must be sensitive to the people around me. I must look at myself—my talents and deficiencies, my background and personal history; I should be present to all these dimensions of my self in prayer. Then the Will of the Father may be revealed to me as I really am. I may see how to make the best of my daily situation. I may sense what He is asking of me. To know the path He wants for me, to follow it faithfully, fills me with joy.

The Lord said He rejoiced in gratefulness that His Father had made known to the simple ones what was hidden from the great and wise. Only the humble find out what God wants them to do with their lives. They harbor no longings for what they cannot be. Such longings are a serious hindrance for the life of the Spirit. They make it difficult for me to find His Will in the only place I can find it—in my daily life with others.

This is the life that is really mine. All other kinds of life may sound interesting, exciting, more fulfilling. He does not want them for me. So I must sacrifice them. However, I may be interested only in sacrificing things I do not like anyway. In that case, my sacrifice has no meaning.

People of the Old Testament sacrificed the best of their crops, the best of their cattle. It might have been painful for them to part with their treasures. Yet they did so wholeheartedly. They did not belittle what they were giving. They did not devalue their gifts to escape the pain of giving.

## ON BEING YOURSELF

I may cling to the possible lives I could have lived by not sacrificing them wholeheartedly. I am an envious giver who begrudges my gift. I look on my gift with a spiteful eye. I do not really give up the lives He asks me to sacrifice. I am secretly preoccupied with lives that cannot be mine. I am filled with resentment. It saps my energy. I cannot be wholly present, as I should be, to my daily reality, for it is here that the Will of the Father shows itself to me. The Spirit of my Lord enlightens me only when I am reading the book of everyday life in reverence and surrender.

Longing for a life that cannot be mine is an obstacle for my spiritual life. Such longing strikes at the root of my life in Christ. In what sense? Blinded by envious preoccupations with other kinds of life, I cannot see what the Will of the Father is for me in my own daily life. I lose track of what my unique life should be like.

The temptation to be something other than what I am called to be is always there. I may give in to unrealistic desires. I may begin to live in fantasy what I cannot live in day to day reality. I become self-alienated, estranged from the Will of the Father for me.

Our Lord himself was often tempted in this way. His public life opened with the story of His temptations in the desert. The tempter pledged Him kingdoms, status, acclaim, lavish nourishment, and service by angels if He would only give up what His

Father asked him to do. As a young boy, He went with His parents to Jerusalem. His Father wanted Him to stay behind with the learned men in the temple. His distraught mother finally found Him. She reproached Him. At that moment He must have felt the pull of the simple wish of a child to be like other children. He could have been that way, of course. And yet, from the viewpoint of His daily life as willed by His Father in Heaven, He could not. He told her that He had to be about the things of His Father.

Later on the temptation to escape His Father's Will came from friends and disciples. He hinted to them that He would suffer and die a shameful death. Some tried to sway Him from his path. They tried to win Him over to their anxious wish that such a thing should not happen to Him. How keenly He must have then felt the temptation for the other kind of life they begged Him to live. It was as if Satan tried to take Him away from His everyday life. In anguish, He beseeched His disciples to go away from Him. He even called one of them Satan. "Get thee hence, Satan." He told His disciples that they only understood the will of man; they did not understand the Will of God for the Son of man.

At the end of His life, that evening in the garden, the temptation again presented itself. Look at the other kinds of life that could have been His. In agony He cried out to the Father to take away from Him the chalice of suffering, to change the course of His life. Yet He affirmed His life as it had to be in the design of His

## ON BEING YOURSELF

Father: "Not mine but your will be done."

How grateful we should be for the example of our Lord. He became like us in everything save sin. Like Him, I should withstand every temptation to leave the everyday life that is willed for me from eternity. He not only gave me His example, He also gave me His Holy Spirit. The Spirit of my Lord is in me as a source of insight. He is in me as a spring of action. He grants me the strength to be faithful to my everydayness and to realize that faithfulness in daily deeds.

## XVII

## TWO KINDS OF WILLING

To will God's Will is to love God. Love is not merely a matter of emotion, sublime experience, or successful comportment. It is first of all a matter of willing. When I say "Your Will be done," I freely give myself to God in love. I become at one with Him in and through my loving will.

I may complain that I cannot feel the same love for God as I feel for husband, wife, or friend. Love is not a matter of what I feel but of what I will. When I say *yes* to everything that God allows in my life, I truly love Him even if I do not feel it.

My union with God, my Origin, resides in the core of myself. At the center of myself is my will. At this center I am free, though many parts of my life may not yield to the lead of my will. It is quite possible that, in spite of my best efforts, my feelings, thoughts, or behavior are at odds with what I would like to be for God. Even my best attempts may prove insufficient to change such deficiencies immediately or ever. What counts, however, is that at the core of myself I am at-one with the Will of God.

I am not responsible for what I cannot change at once or perhaps may never be able to change. My will to be at-one with the Divine Will is what matters. If the radiance of my transformed will is able to touch and change the other dimensions of my personal life, all the better. Were I in that case to refuse the possible transformation of my life, it would be a clear indication that I am not truly willing the Divine Will. My good will implies that I try to transform my life in the light of His Will, so far as this is possible.

On the other hand, the Divine Will also includes that I accept in peace the limits of my possibilities of self-transformation. My limits too are willed by God's allowing Will.

*What Willing Means*

I may feel uneasy when I hear that the loving union with my Origin is a matter of willing. The cause of this uneasiness may be confusion in regard to the word "willing." To clarify what willing means, we can make a distinction between two kinds of willing: the will as fundamental self-orientation and the will as concrete embodiment and execution of this self-orientation.

My will as self-orientation refers to my most fundamental freedom. There is nothing violent or forceful about this central kind of willing. I as willing in this sense tend quietly toward that which I come to know as valuable or loveable. To will the Will of God is thus first of all a relaxed tending of my free self towards Him and towards what seems to be His Will in a certain life situation.

The second kind of willing, the executive will, is different. It refers to my attempt to make concrete in daily life the value to which I have oriented my self. For example, I am a man who loves his family dearly. This is not to say that I necessarily feel this love at all times. I may be so aggravated by my wife's nagging, my children's disobedience, the weekly bills, the computation of my income tax that it is impossible for me to *feel* very loving. Feeling love, however, is not the point. I truly love my family because I truly will their well being. I really will that more than anything else in my life.

To will the well being of my family is first of all a free fundamental orientation of my self towards my family. In some instances, willing their well being may be nothing more than just that. Imagine if I were in an accident that paralyzed me from the waist down. I could do relatively little to implement my self-orientation toward the well being of my family in concrete action that would further their interests. This does not mean that I do not love them or that I do not have their well being at heart.

Or take another situation. What if by temperament I were easily upset and angry? I have a terrible day at the office; driving home I have a minor accident that wrecks the fender of my car. Upon arriving home, my kids behave badly and my wife, tired from her own day, begins to nag me. At this moment, it may be impossible for me to express my loving self-orientation towards the family in tender words and feelings. Whether I like it or not, I find myself feeling and speaking in a tired and irritated way. This incident illustrates that I cannot always embody the orientation of my primary will in concrete acts and feelings.

Even when I can express my will in concrete life, I must often cope with resistances. People, events, and things do not automatically yield to my self-orientation. Neither do my own thoughts, feelings, and habits spontaneously comply with what I will. Perceptions, feelings, memories, imaginations, customs, and habits—all may rebel against the self-orientation of my will. To overcome such resistances, I have to exert effort. In this secondary phase of willing, I would be wise to exert only as much effort as necessary to overcome the resistance.

My expenditure of effort and energy should also be guided by other factors. I should not over-exert myself. I should not be so eager to obtain an immediate success that I harm health of mind or body or destroy my emotional balance. I should not be so violent in my executive willing that I upset people around me unnecessarily. In that case I may do more harm than good.

Remember God's allowing Will speaks also in the resistances I meet in life. The same Divine Will speaks, moreover, in the limits of mind and body as well as those of my life situation. It is thus God's Will that my executive willing takes these limits into account.

*Problem of Executive Willing*

With these two kinds of willing in mind, we can now return to our original question: Why is it that I feel uneasy to say that my love for God is the same as my willing of the Divine Will? One reason is that I am inclined to identify all willing with executive willing. Furthermore I am tempted to see the essence of this executive willing as violent over-exertion. This reaction is due at least in part to the culture in which I am living.

Western culture has promoted secondary executive willing often at the cost of primary self-orientation. This culture places a high premium on practical performance and achievement. One of the guiding forces of this achievement mentality is competition. I must try to outdo my neighbor. This competitive stance inclines me to exert myself over and beyond my reasonable limits. As a result, the word "willing" may have for me an unpleasant connotation of force. It reminds me of painful, unreasonable demands for self-exertion, of desperate competition, of fearing ever to fail.

Such exclusive use of the secondary will and its constant over-exertion is precisely the opposite of what is meant by willing in the spiritual life. In my spiritual life, willing is a matter of relaxed self-orientation towards my mysterious Origin from which I emerge constantly. When and if I discover what the Will of God is in a certain situation, I tend toward that Will in loving self-orientation. This is a first step. Then the secondary aspect of my willing may come into play.

Genuine willing implies that I try to make the Divine Will come true in my real situation. I quietly exert myself, willing to overcome the resistances I meet there. My exertion never becomes over-exertion. As a spiritual person, I expend effort but this effort is always marked by moderation and the maintenance of equanimity. I realize that the Will of God is expressed not only in this or that concrete effect to be realized but also in the way in which I respond to His Will. My response to the Father's Will is always deeply respectful of all other expressions of His Will, especially as it speaks in my bodily, psychological, emotional, and spiritual limitations.

I should remove from the expression "to love God is to will the Will of God" any connotation of undue stress, violence, and compulsiveness. In this regard, I should follow the example of our Lord, who obeyed the Will of the Father in a non-violent way. I should become at-one with my Lord: "But whoever is joined to the Lord becomes one spirit with him" (1 Cor. 6:17).

To accept the will of God in a relaxed way, is to love God and to love Him is to be at-one with Him. This repeated at-oneness makes me more and more like Him.

*Christ as Model of Willing Out of Love*

When Christ came into the world, He expressed the

whole meaning of His life in these words: "Then I said, 'As is written of me in the book, I have come to do your will, O God.' " (Hebrews 10:7). This attitude shaped His life, directed His movement and inspired His thoughts, feelings, and deeds. His life was a song of praise to the Father—a joyful abiding by the Divine Will.

To do the Will of the Father was not only the content of His life but also the center of His teachings on spirituality. "None of those who cry out, 'Lord, Lord,' will enter the kingdom of God but only the one who does the will of my Father in heaven" (Mt. 7:21). "Whoever does the will of my heavenly Father is brother and sister and mother to me" (Mt. 12:50). He was so at-one with His Divine Origin that He did only what pleased His Father. "The One who sent me is with me. He has not deserted me since I always do what pleases Him" (John 8:29). "Doing the will of him who sent me and bringing his work to completion is my food" (John 4:34).

The Lord was not eager to please Himself or others. The only thing to consider was the Will of the Father. He said to His parents who were searching for Him in sorrow when He stayed behind in the temple, "Why did you search for me? Did you not know I had to be in my Father's house?" (Lk. 2:49).

Our Savior went to His sacred Passion deeply immersed in the Will of His Father. ". . .but the world must know that I love the Father and do as the Father has commanded me. Come, then! Let us be on our way" (John 14:31). Then in the garden, suffering the agony of His coming passion and death, He prayed three times: "My Father, if it is possible, let this cup pass me by. Still, let it be as you would have it, not as I" (Mt. 26:39). He remained faithful to the Father's Will until His last moment. ". . .obediently accepting even death, death on a cross!" (Phil. 2:8).

A meditative reading of the Gospel and the letters of the apostles cannot but convince me that the center of my spirituality should be to embrace the Will of the Father as Christ did. To fulfill the Will of God is to live in divine worship all day long. Thus to conform myself to the Will of the Father is the most fundamental way of spirituality given to me as a Christian.

# XVIII

## GOD'S WILL AND MY ORIGINAL LIMITS

To accept God's Will is to accept the original limits of my life.

Let us say that I am the father of a large family; my income is modest. This means I am faced with certain limits. I cannot spend as much money as I would like to for food and entertainment. I can look at these limits merely from the viewpoint of needs that cannot be fulfilled. I might in this case feel angry and rebellious. Or I could fall into the opposite attitude. I might become indifferent. I do not face my limits creatively by working for change in my situation.

In both cases, I experience limits as confining. In my anger and rebellion, I am like a prisoner who bangs his head against the walls of his cell. In my indifference, I am like a caged animal that no longer cares about its confinement.

As spirit, however, I see my limits in a creative way. They are for me a challenge and an invitation. In them I see the Divine Will that allows for the emergence of these circumstances. In and through them, my original life must unfold itself. A too modest income is neither cause for blind rebellion nor occasion for mute resignation. My life situation is not seen as a static prison that pens me in but as an ever changing field for exploration.

The limit of a modest income, for example, is not seen as limiting once and for all my personal potential. Rather I see this limit as a divine challenge to make the best of whatever income I have by careful economizing. This kind of attention demands effort on my part. Still I do it in a relaxed manner, knowing that stretching my money is one way I can respond to the challenge of the Divine Will in my life today.

Adoring God's allowing Will helps me to avoid the resentment which would hinder harmonious self-unfolding. If I were bitter, not only would my family be deprived of some material things; worse than this, they would be denied the presence of a father whose love for them is not poisoned by resentment.

Adoring the Divine Will in every event of daily life thus prevents the development of a despondent life style. It also fosters personal growth. If I answer the invitation of a modest income by trying out of love for God to make the best of my situation, I will engage many of my abilities. I have to plan ahead carefully, be inventive in buying groceries, compensate creatively for the lack of costly entertainment. Doing these things is nothing new or spectacular. Spiritual life does not consist in doing extraordinary things; it is the fulfillment of everyday responsibilities out of love for God. Such an attitude makes these cares fruitful for my spiritual growth.

*Many Answers to His Will*

Many responses can be given to the inviting Will of God. What answer I choose depends partly on my originality, partly on my life situation. God deeply respects my human freedom and leaves room for me to choose freely from many answers that will equally well fulfill His Holy Will.

To follow the Will of God does not mean, therefore, to live in blind conformity to the limits of my life. For example, I may be limited by a crippling disease like arthritis. I could say, "My incapacity is God's Will," and give up any attempt to move and act, not even considering ways of responding creatively to the limits He allowed in my life. Such deadening apathy is not only unspiritual; it is decidedly inhuman.

*Compulsive and Hysterical Reactions to His Will*

One subhuman reaction to my limits would be *compulsive* conformity to only one meaning, excluding all other possibilities. For example, in the case of a too modest salary, I may live in the mistaken notion that the only response to God's Will is to accept my salary without doing anything to improve it. I feel compelled to repeat rigidly to myself, "To do God's Will means not to complain about my salary" or "God's Will means that I am not to fight with others for social justice."

This may indeed be the best answer to God's Will

for a certain type of person in a certain situation. To come to this decision, however, presupposes consideration of other possibilities in relaxed and playful freedom. In other words, God's Will as embodied in the limits of my life situation is first of all a divine invitation to weigh all possible answers.

I may respond to a limit in my life with an equally subhuman *hysterical* reaction, restricting myself again to one exclusive meaning of the situation. In hysterical obedience to what I call God's Will, I am spellbound by only one "exciting" meaning of the situation proposed to me by my own fantasy or by enthusiastic fellowmen as *the only* meaning. In the case of a too modest salary, a group of people suffering the same plight may tell me excitedly that the only answer to God's will is to engage in protest demonstrations. Their agitation is contagious. As a matter of fact, this may be the best answer to His Will for certain types of people in certain situations. It is by no means sure that I am this type of person. Prayerful reflection may tell me whether this answer is best for me. I should never do things simply because I am overwhelmed by the enthusiasm of others. Mine would then not be a free response but an hysterical reaction. It would not help me to grow in the spiritual life.

Compulsive and hysterical reactions may appear pious in their motivation and expression. Nevertheless they paralyze the life of man as original spirit. When my prayers are compulsive, a forced piety may begin to rule my life. When hysterical, an exalted religiosity may color each expression of spirituality. Both styles of following the Will of God are subhuman because both responses are unfree.

## Divine Respect for Human Originality

Blind exaltation or mindless conformity usually bypass the core of God's Will for me. He first of all wants me to choose freely how to best obey His Will, for He created me. From eternity He willed me as an original spirit distinct from animals and plants which have built-in reactions to stimuli. At times I may feel like falling back to the subhuman level of reaction. I may envy the unconcerned existence of animals and plants. They do not have to ponder before they respond. They are not burdened with responsibility. Under the pretext of a false piety, I may become wholly passive. Mere passivity, however, destroys the original life of the Spirit and makes spiritual growth impossible.

My uncreative response may alienate others. They feel repelled by my so-called "doing the Will of God." I look dead and uninspired to them. Either that or I come across to them as so fanatic, so one-sidedly absorbed in emotional enthusiasm, that I turn them off. If this is what it means to do the Will of God, then it is not for us, they will say. Rightly they feel that neither the mindless nor the willful way of doing things is faithful to our humanity.

## His Will Is Invitation

For the spiritual man limits are invitations. God's

Will is not a military command: "Do it this way and no questions asked." Neither is His situated Will a direct order; it is a gentle invitation to ponder the many ways in which I can respond to the situation facing me; to see this situation from all sides; to discover in it the variety of meanings it can have for me and other people.

His Will is an invitation to decide freely which meaning and response seems best to me in light of my limited insight here and now. I may discover later in life that my answer was not the best one objectively. It was, however, one of the possible answers I, with my limited insight, could give at that time. Therefore, I was truly following the Will of God. The same Divine Will, which allowed this specific life situation to occur, allowed also for my insight to be as limited as it was at the time.

Certain choices were ruled out from the beginning. I could not choose a response clearly at odds with the laws of God and their unfolding explanation by His Church. I could not choose a response that went against my fundamental make-up, for this make-up is a more primordial expression of God's will for me than my actual situation. For the same reason I could not choose a response that unnecessarily harmed the fundamental make-up of others.

I must thus avoid two extremes. One extreme is to forgo all reflection, that is, to take one possible meaning of the situation as the *only* possible meaning and call this the Will of God. Such an exclusive response may simply be a first emotional reaction or a suggestion by some powerful person or group. The other extreme is to respond to the situation with any arbitrary whim that strikes my fancy at the moment.

In answer to God's Will, I first of all eliminate any response that is at odds with other revelations of God in His Church or in my original vital, familial, and cultural make-up. My spiritual growth secondly presupposes that I have the relaxed patience to evaluate all sides of the given situation and to consult with others if that would prove helpful. Only then can I decide what God's Will seems to be for me at this moment.

This is the usual way of developing my spiritual life in answer to God's Will. I know from the history of the saints, however, that God can break through the veil of daily appearances. He might reveal His Will for a man's original life suddenly and unmistakenly. The conversion of St. Paul on his way to Damascus is an example. In such an exceptional case, there is no need to ponder the possibility of all kinds of other answers. I should not even be concerned about my vital, familial, and cultural background. In such a moment the revelation of God is so clear that I know at once what He wants me to do. Nevertheless, if something so exceptional would ever happen to me, it would be wise to consult a spiritual director and—depending on the issue at stake—the authorities in the Church. For I am always in danger of self-deception and illusion.

# XIX

## ORIGINAL FAITHFULNESS TO THE DIVINE WILL

The will of my Father in heaven speaks to me in the simple challenge of everyday life. This Divine Will made itself known in the same way in the daily life of Jesus. Never shall I be as sensitive and loyal to the Will of the Father as Jesus was. He surrendered Himself wholly to the Divine Will. He was so at-one with the Divine Will that this Will became transparent in Him.

In the same spirit of my Lord, I must try to respond to the Will of the Father. This is the only way to unfold the fullness of my divine originality. There is no greater act of divine worship than daily fidelity to the Will of God. This faithfulness should be my main concern. I should first seek the Kingdom of God's Will in my life. All the rest will then be given to me. I do not have to be concerned, for my fidelity to Him cannot outdo His fidelity to me.

Even before the creation of the world, God the Father saw my life in its smallest detail. No hair falls from my head without His knowledge (Mt. 10:30). All the unique circumstances that steadily emerge and disappear in my life, like the rising and falling waves of the sea, have been allowed by Him, not in indifference but in tender concern. "We are truly his handiwork, created in Christ Jesus to lead the life of good deeds which God prepared for us in advance" (Eph. 2:10).

I may not comprehend His ways for me. "How deep are the riches and the wisdom and the knowledge of God! How inscrutable his judgments, how unsearchable his ways! For 'who has known the mind of the Lord? Or who has been his counselor?' . . ." (Rom. 11:33-35).

Deep down I may feel that nobody is more concerned about me than I myself. And yet God's love for me is so much deeper than my love for myself; He takes my interest to heart much more than I could ever do. With infinite care, He takes into account the most hidden aspects of my unique self. His loving attention penetrates into the most secret needs of my personality, needs which are unknown to myself. What He allows in my life flows forth from His love for me.

The Divine Will is gentle and generous in all things, never ungracious or miserly. Whatever affects me inwardly or outwardly—be it from my own original make-up and personal history or from people, events, and things, it is the Will of God.

This Will invites me to search for my own limited response to all that happens to me. He asks me to give the best response I can. I should gladly accept His invitation, convinced that I can do nothing better with my life. I cannot worship God in any better manner than by accepting each particular moment and incident as a divine invitation to creative thought and action.

Yet I must not be so naive as to feel that my original answers in and by themselves are that worthwhile. God is the origin of my finite originality. He Himself makes it possible for my small performance to originate from me. "For from him and through him and for him all things are" (Rom. 11:36).

There is thus no greater thing I can do than to be faithful to the Will of God in the most simple events of daily life. The common things of everyday I must do in an uncommon way. I do them in loving union with the Divine Will. It may sometimes be easier to do great things than little ones. The grandeur of an enterprise, the excitement of a splendid project, the interest and admiration of others carry me forward. I feel successful, important, liked, needed. Mesmerized by the praises of men, I may become spellbound by applause—so much so that I no longer hear the voice of my original calling. Bewitched by the projects of people, I become estranged from God's original Will for me. Spoiled by success, I become self-alienated in the deepest sense.

True spiritual life shows itself most convincingly in faithfulness to God in the smallest events. These things cannot earn me recognition from others. They are too small to be noticed.

The nature of tasks to which I am called by predisposition and personal history is not that important. My performances may be great or small, hidden or public, humble or exalted. It does not

matter. The only thing that counts is that the Eternal wills it. There is no need for further concern. What matters is my surrender to God's loving Will. If I am called to greater things, however, I should remind myself that the path of greatness is not the safest path spiritually for man.

The best preparation for fidelity to the Divine Will in uncommon things is faithfulness to His Will in the commonality of everyday life. Perhaps this is the reason for the hidden life of Jesus. God became man only once. Surprisingly He spent most of His life as an unknown carpenter in a forgotten village. His fellow villagers were astounded to the point of indignation when this quiet craftsman, at the end of His life, began to speak up in public. Irritated, they asked each other, "Is that not the son of the carpenter whose father and mother we know?" When He kept appearing in public, they sincerely thought that this simple son of the carpenter must have gone mad. In genuine concern, they tried to take Him away from His listeners, to bring Him back home where He hopefully would calm down and take up again the everyday chores He was accustomed to.

He spent only a few short years in public life. Even then He took off at times to hide Himself from the people.

God chose the simple life. Think of the marvelous books He could have written, the astounding art He could have created, the political wonders He could have performed as a social leader of a racial minority. Think

of the housing projects He as a master craftsman could have developed for the poor in cities like Jerusalem. What He could have done for the underprivileged in the Roman superstate. He could have been a successful social agitator for human rights.

He chose instead to pass almost all of His life as an unnoticed carpenter in a little forgotten village. God became man only once. Why did He choose to live most of this life in the grayness of everyday service? For what other reason than to give me an example of the way in which I can sanctify myself in the quiet living of a simple life?

Are not most of us called to a hidden existence like that of Jesus? The Divine Master gave me, therefore, an example of a day-to-day spiritual life lived within the limits of an unpretentious homespun situation.

It is often difficult to accept the challenges in my life as God's invitation. People may undermine me by slanderous words, malicious actions, mean insinuations. It is difficult to see God's Will in that. Their behavior is sinful, at least objectively; God must loathe their sin. So should I. But the painful effects of their faults, I must accept as allowed by the Divine Will. Human opposition is a divine challenge to be met wisely and courageously in my own original way.

Faith will help me to resent less that God allows such unpleasant and tiring challenges to emerge in my life. Only faith can teach me not to resent the output of energy, creativity, and tactful attention each opposition demands from me.

God did not approve of the harshness of the people of Bethlehem. But for Mary and Joseph the dire effects of their indifference were an invitation of God to cope with these consequences creatively. They sought and found a stable and a manger; they tried to make the best of the situation in accordance with their own original make-up and insight. They creatively converted the manger into a cradle; they inventively changed pieces of linen into swaddling clothes.

God was not pleased with the criminal persecution by Herod. The Holy Family accepted in faith that the consequent danger for the life of their child was allowed by God. For them it was again a divinely allowed challenge to cope with creatively. The cautious flight to Egypt, the creative work of bodily and spiritual survival in the midst of a pagan civilization, was their courageous and intelligent answer.

The furious opposition of the Pharisees and the high priests to Jesus did not have God's approval. His Will allowed the consequent challenge for our Lord to defend Himself and His teachings by debating with them wisely and fearlessly. Again His life reminds me that "We know that God makes all things work together for the good of those who have been called according to his decree" (Rom. 8:28).

## XX

## UNION WITH GOD AND TRANSFORMATION OF SELF

I must become at-one with God by becoming at-one with His original plan for me. I am already in Him and of Him from the beginning as one of His unique creations. But, as I grow, I must become transformed into a living expression of what He uniquely wanted me to be from eternity. Finding my originality is a homecoming to the Eternal.

My life as a whole has to be transformed. The main agent of this transformation is my graced will. But my will can influence my life only to a degree. Often I have no direct say over my moods, thoughts, actions, and feelings. Many times they elude my freedom. I may succeed in transforming some of them slowly and gradually with God's Grace. A final purification and transformation will be granted to me only in the hereafter.

Once I am transformed to the unique design that God intended for me from the beginning, I will be able to be wholly at-one with Him. I will experience my personal eternal union with Him, as it was intended for me in a way different from that of anyone else's. I will have been cleansed by God Himself from all foreign accretions that were not me. I will have reached the radiant clarity of God's unique word as spoken in and through His Eternal Word, that unique word that is me.

During this life I shall not achieve full purification of· my whole being—acts, thoughts, and feelings. Foreign accretions, accumulated from infancy on, may already be too many to overcome in a lifetime. My good will is all that counts for Him. If I fully *will* the purity of His original design in my life, I become at-one with Him, if not in the whole of my person, at least in the root of my being, my free will.

To will His design implies that I improve in myself what I can improve. For example, I may have developed an unreasonable hostility toward some people. I may be unaware of the depth of this hidden resentment, which may have emerged in childhood. Rightly or wrongly I felt I was mistreated by the grown-ups around me. I felt enraged. As a small child, dependent on their power, I was too scared to show my anger. I did not even dare to admit to myself how badly I felt. I was afraid of the constant feeling of my furiousness; it might betray itself to them. This discovery, I dreaded, could be the end of me. Therefore, I repressed the awareness of my anger. I did not do this willfully or conceptually. It took place in me as an instinctive, unreasoned way of controlling inner feelings that frightened me. After some time of repression, I no longer realized this bursting rage inside me.

Now this pent-up rage tends to cling to people I meet in daily life. For example, I feel more disgusted with difficult colleagues than others do, but I don't know why. Unaware of my rage that has never been worked through, I may fancy that my irritation is justified by their unpleasant attitude. My dislike, however, is out of proportion to their idiosyncrasies. Others are bothered by their unpleasant attitude too, but not with the same intensity as I. They seem more able to see their good features, and often find grounds to excuse their offensive ways. My dislike must be rooted in a hidden resentment of which I am unaware. This resentment has become so much a part of my personality that I may be tempted to see it as the original me. I may say, "That's the way I'm made. What can I do about it?"

This resentment does not belong to the original me, however. Resentment is not an expression of temperament. A violent temperamental reaction may be typical of one's vital make-up, but resentment is not the result of temperament. Nobody is born with resentment. Resentment and its repression began when I felt that I could not express safely an overwhelming anxiety, rage, or indignation evoked in me by others.

I do not know about this past deformation of my personality. I hence cannot purify myself of it. Neither can I consecrate this unpurified dimension of my original being to God.

Later in life this or any other hidden dimension may become known to me. Spiritual direction, counseling, psychotherapy, meditation, spiritual reading, a lecture, or a talk with a friend may make me aware of something in myself that needs to be changed. This hidden dimension then becomes available to my will. My will alone cannot spiritualize such defects totally. God's Grace is needed. I must cooperate with that Grace. I-as-graced-willing must transform and consecrate my life. As St. Augustine says in one of his sermons, "He that created you without your knowledge, will not save you without your consent."

My graced will consecrates, spiritualizes, and divinizes my life. By my graced-willing, I begin to change into the original person I was meant to be from eternity. My graced will consecrates those thoughts, feelings, and actions that increasingly become available to my self-understanding and freedom; it permeates what is human in me with the divine. My will also consecrates all that God asks me to do whether I work as artist or farmer, intellectual or manual laborer, employee or administrator. In every place and moment, I surrender creatively to the challenges the Divine Will allows in my daily life.

I as willing must consecrate each moment of my life. No room should be left for morbid concern about past or future. What matters is the present and only those aspects of past or future that are directly relevant to the effective living of this moment. The present moment is the sacrament of the Divine Will here and now. I should give myself wholly to it. As Jesus said, "Whoever puts his hand to the plow but keeps looking back is unfit for the reign of God" (Lk. 9:62). I should thus not look back unnecessarily while doing the Will of God here and now. Neither should I be too concerned about the future. "Cast your care upon the Lord, and he will support you . . ." (Ps. 55:23).

Often I worry about all kinds of things that could go wrong. Because of my worries, I miss the actual moment. I may break down under the strain of imagined misfortunes that might happen to me. I cannot expect to receive the Grace now to bear problems that are not yet bothering me or that have no relevance to my present effectiveness. I can be assured of the graces necessary to live this moment of my life in response to God's Will. The best care is, in a sense, not to care. The greatest wisdom is to celebrate gratefully the time I live in now.

Creative collaboration with the Divine Will as permeating the present moment increases my strength, wisdom, and depth of experience. I will carry this increase in grace, skill, force, and insight to the next moment. This new challenge of God's Will, when lived to the full, will again enrich and deepen me. I will keep growing from strength to strength, from insight to insight, from grace to grace. No preparation can be more effective to ready me for the challenges of life that will come my way in later days.

The whole mystery of unfolding nature, culture, and history flows forth continuously from the loving Will of God. His saving wisdom permeates the most myriad details. My life is a tiny fragment of this mysterious whole, a passing wave in the divine sea. I can never know exactly how I am woven into the fabric of Divine Willing, which allows past, future, and present to run their mysterious course. The one thing that matters is my relaxed attempt to live each moment of life in presence to His Will.

In spite of the time and energy I spend in prayer, spiritual reading, mortification, and charitable endeavors, I may find that I do not grow spiritually. The reason may be that "I" am too much in the foreground, too busy, too preoccupied with the success of my personal and spiritual growth. In a sense I care too much. The best care would be to let God care for me. To say, "I know, my Lord, that countless ways can lead to you. But out of all these ways, you in your love have willed one way for me. You alone know the original way that will be mine. To me you reveal that way step by step. I cannot know, as you, how each step is linked to the step before and to the steps you will ask me to take hereafter. Sometimes I lose my path, but you always wait for me with an infinite patience. You are the shepherd who returns me steadily to my pasture. Help me to be present in the simplicity of my heart to each original place and moment along the way you have laid out for me."

To be holy means to be wholly in the present, not to look backward or forward exclusively but to be fully in the given moment.

A Japanese monk related the following parable to his disciples.

A man was traveling along a road and saw coming

toward him a tiger. He ran the other way, but the tiger ran after him. The man reached a ravine. Hanging down in the ravine was the root of a tree. He caught this root and let himself down over the edge. The tiger sniffed at him from the edge. Terrified the man looked below him and saw another tiger there. His life depended on the root of the tree. Some mice began to gnaw at the root. At that moment the man discovered a delicious strawberry. He held the root with one hand; with the other he plucked the strawberry. *How delicious the strawberry tasted.* The tigers were forgotten.

This degree of forgetfulness in the face of mortal danger is foreign to us who live an incarnated Christian spirituality, in which human feelings are not so easily forgotten. Nevertheless, I still can learn a lesson from this story that ties in with what we have reflected upon; namely, the value of being fully present to the things that are offered to me at this moment of my life.

Someone said to Jesus: "I will be your follower, Lord, but first let me take leave of my people at home." Jesus answered him: "Whoever puts his hand to the plow but keeps looking back is unfit for the reign of God" (Lk. 9:61-62). St. Paul writes to the Philippians, "I give no thought to what lies behind but push on to what is ahead. My entire attention is on the finish line as I run toward the prize to which God calls me—life on high in Christ Jesus. All of us who are spiritually mature must have this attitude" (Phil. 3:13-15). In my fidelity to the Divine Will, I must not be hindered by my past. I must shake off any morbid preoccupation with former faults and failures. Otherwise I waste my energy worrying about what has been and I miss the joy and equanimity that makes me available for the relaxed and creative fulfillment of God's Will here and now. The gloomy spectre of past sins should not haunt me. I cannot save myself; neither can I render satisfaction for my infidelities. Christ alone is my Redeemer. He washes away the stain of sin. "Though your sins be like scarlet, they may become white as snow; though they may be crimson red, they may become white as wool" (Isaiah 1:18). " . . . but despite the increase of sin, grace has far surpassed it" (Rom. 5:20).

God is not a compulsive bookkeeper who constantly adds up my faults and failures. He is not a small-minded ruler who cannot forget an insult after repentance has been done and forgiveness has been granted. "Their sins and their transgressions I will remember no more" (Heb. 10:17). God wants me to turn away from everything in the past that is not relevant to the present challenge. He wants me to celebrate this moment as a precious invitation of His Will. What He forgives is forgiven forever. Nothing is more fully done away with than the infidelities which God has forgiven.

It may thus be difficult for me to be creatively present to the invitation of God's Will if I live too much in the past and too little in the present. I may waste my vitality carrying around useless burdens. Tormenting myself with the memories of past mistakes robs me of the undivided strength I need for the challenge of the moment. I miss the equanimity that makes me more receptive to the Divine Grace which is given to me here and now.

In a spiritual sense, I should be a man without a past, a man of today. The future should not terrify me; the past should not trouble me. I should live only in the holy temple of this graced moment. I should bless this original tiny fraction of eternity granted to me now. When any worry over repented sins emerges, I should remember: "For with the Lord is kindness and with him is plenteous redemption . . . " (Ps. 130:7).

**XXI**

## ORIGINALITY AND THE FOLLOWING OF CHRIST

My originality
is hidden with Christ in God. In Him, the Eternal Word,
I am immersed as a tiny unique word spoken by the
Eternal for one small moment in time and space.

The Eternal Word became a man like me. He shows
me in the flesh how to respond to the Will of the
Father, how to become the original word the Father
wants me to be. He invites me to follow Him.

How I follow Him depends on who I am. My original
calling enables me to experience as personally
meaningful those aspects of the life of Jesus that are in
tune with my mission in life. They speak to me as I am.
Therefore I can imitate them more easily.

The life and words of Jesus can be understood in
many ways. All of them may be enlightening; but not
all of His ways will be equally enlightening for me. My
eternal originality is a light that I spontaneously bring
to the story of the life of the Lord. My originality is like
a lamp in which this message lights up for me uniquely.
Each man carries the light of his own originality. Each
man therefore experiences the Gospel in a somewhat
different way.

## ON BEING YOURSELF

The more I discover my unique eternal calling, the more the light of my uniqueness will reveal to me the special meaning of the Lord's life for me. In this light, I may discover meanings and attitudes that are truly there but that I did not see before. I may understand these aspects of His life better than some because of who I uniquely am. For the same reason some of my fellow Christians may understand other aspects better than I because of who they uniquely are.

Jesus' life is not a restricting stereotype. Each one must follow Him in his own way. In this following, he will discover Jesus in a personal way, a way infinitely meaningful for Him.

I must attempt to live my original life in the light of the Lord without losing my originality or betraying His message. Part of my originality, as many of these reflections have revealed, is due to vital make-up, family background, culture, and the unique everyday situations I have to face. Part of the original life of Jesus was a first century oriental culture, a somewhat rustic family life, an environment of small town people, craftsmen, and fishermen. Later He spoke in simple parables that at first sight may not seem to apply to the complex situations with which I have to cope in an over-organized, sophisticated civilization.

Christ calls Himself the way. If He is the way, I ought to follow Him. He is also the light, which should enlighten my life. I should cultivate, as St. Paul says, the spirit of Christ: "Since we live by the spirit, let us follow the spirit's lead" (Gal. 5:25).

My imitation of Him must nonetheless be an original imitation—true both to my self and to His example. I cannot simply mimic Christ as stylized by one or the other cultural period, nationality, preacher, or spiritual writer. My following of Christ ought not to be necessarily and precisely as others have seen and described Him. Their experience of the Lord may have been most meaningful to them and to their contemporaries, who shared spontaneously the same feeling and vision. They met the Lord in a role that made sense to them. After them others may have taken over their presentation without personal feeling and reflection. Their picture of Christ may then have deteriorated into a set of cliché postures. I can only become my true self, however, if my life is anchored not to the ways in which others saw the Lord but to my own experience of Him.

To be myself means that I allow to unfold in me that inner something that can make me come to life as a unique person. What little selfhood I have may be stunted. If I have lost the courage to be myself, it is in and through my attempt to follow the Lord that I may be restored to selfhood.

Nobody—not even myself—can have as deep a respect as Jesus does for the private mystery and elusive dynamics of my interior life. The Lord has an infinite divine reverence for my radical originality. My personal meeting with Him, therefore, will lead to the full flowering of my uniqueness.

My true self may be stunted. If I do not participate

in the radical respect of Jesus for my unique calling and responsibility, my self- awakening may be arrested. I may be satisfied with a partially developed self, comfortable and mediocre, a respectable but dull self, trivialized by daily gossip and the little schemes for prestige, power, and possession.

Without Christ's radical example, I may do good only when I see some advantage in it for myself. I may give of myself only in an attempt to gain the appreciation and good will of others. Instead of becoming a follower of Jesus, I follow the worldly opinions of some establishment, organization, movement, or crowd. Instead of becoming a Christ-directed man, I become a world-directed man, a superficial cheerleader, a mere regular fellow. Without the enlightening example of my Lord's life, I may squander and lose my own.

Through all the deeds and teachings of Jesus, there resounds one simple theme, that of awakening. He wants me to repent and convert from what the world wants me to be to what God wants me to be. I cannot reflect on the words of Jesus and avoid the shock of self-recognition. This shock is a grace. Presence to His words will compel me to reexamine my life and its motivations. I will feel inspired to hide my life in His.

To be hidden in Christ is to be taken out of the world that has drugged my original self with cheap instant satisfactions. I may have lulled myself into mediocrity by taking in like a sponge the suggestions of public media, movements, and crowds. To be hidden in Christ is to live in the penetrating light of His original life. His life awakens me to that self-awareness and evaluation that must precede and accompany personal presence to God.

The following of Christ implies two main things. On the one hand, I follow Him in accordance with my original self. This side of my imitation guides the original "how" of my following. On the other hand, the same imitation, enlightened and graced by the Holy Spirit, enhances and transforms my human originality. It is no longer a merely human originality. In the sight of God, my original self gains a Christ-like beauty and value by its immersion in the life of His beloved Son. Ultimately, in and through Christ, my human self becomes in some way a divinized self.

As long as my originality has not been graced by this transformation, it remains a truncated originality; it has not yet found its infinite origin in and through the Eternal Word in whom it was created.

## *Transformation in Christ*

Originality transformed in Christ is the deepest originality I can live. Immersed in Christ, I will live the paradox of being most at-one with God and most aware of my uniqueness and aloneness before God. I will be less tempted to escape from the divine mystery of my life by losing myself in the crowd of regular fellows. Christ's life will be a constant reminder to me that I cannot follow Him and at the same time drift through life never reflecting on my own uniqueness.

The Eternal Word became man and walked here on earth to enable me to encounter Him in the flesh. He came to this earth not merely to pronounce some mysterious sentences for the interest of learned exegetes. He came to live an original life before God so that I might learn from Him. The center of my spiritual life must be, therefore, the original living of my everyday existence in the light of the life of Jesus.

To help me to find my true self concretely, Jesus lived a common life. He was at-home in the familiar world in which I live—the world of simple celebrations, of sickness and death, of small talk and gossip, of food, weather, friends, families, houses, travel. He was caught up in the everyday cares of men. He met people we all meet—gentle and crude, outcasts and men who have made it socially, saintly persons, sinners, and prostitutes, greedy, hospitable, vacillating, and loyal people. He had to find his way through a tangle of temptations, to make far reaching decisions on His own. He suffered slander, betrayal, false trial, public insult, scourging, and violent death.

The Jesus I must follow is thus not a shadow, a poetic visionary, or a floating image. He was like me in everything but sin. Therefore, my original following of the words of Christ must be inspired by the way in which these words were spoken—in plain talk with concrete men in their earthly and human environment. I should not pry His words loose from their mundane everyday context. Jesus spoke spontaneously to real life situations. He did not dictate an abstract outline of ideas, a general system of life to be commented upon by scholarly men. He lived a concrete life to be followed by all people, learned and simple alike.

Once I truly accept the invitation of Jesus to follow Him, I will never be free from His relentless Presence. The life of Jesus will reproach me when I pursue the gratification of my false self, when I want the comfortable life style of the regular fellow who follows the crowd in his eagerness to be liked. Such an alienated life style collides with the demands of Jesus. It is difficult to follow Him because it is difficult to bear the solitude of my original calling in Christ. If Christianity would consist only in affirming a set of certified phrases, it would be an easy religion. But Christianity as the day to day imitation of Christ is quite a different matter.

## *Originality and Imitation*

Original imitation cannot be a reduplication of the life of Jesus. In that case it would not be my life. Even if I would try to, I could not reduplicate the originality of His existence. He is the only Son of the Father; His life was without fault or failure; His Will was perfectly in tune with the Divine Will. It would be blasphemous even to think that I could try to match that.

Original imitation excludes strict conformity; it implies creative adaptation of the attitudes of Jesus to my original givenness and my unique situation. Such imitation must be in tune with the Voice of the Father who speaks in my vital, familial, cultural, and actual self. This Divine Voice conveys a unique message to each Christian. Therefore, the attempts of various Christians, who sincerely try to follow Jesus, may lead to different choices, actions, and life styles. Each follower of Christ retains his astounding, inaccessible God-given uniqueness. To become a follower of Christ can thus never mean that I force my self into a fixed mold.

There are many ways of allowing the original Christian life to emerge. The way I follow must respect the rich and mysterious originality of my unique sojourn in time and space. No simple scheme of behavior, no set of fixed prescriptions, can do justice to an original following of Jesus.

Following Him means first of all to immerse myself in the inner attitudes of Jesus toward the Father, toward the world, and toward other people. These attitudes come to life for me in His words and deeds as presented in the Gospels. I should meditate on them often, asking myself what they may mean for me in my unique situation. Then I must ask myself how I can incorporate these attitudes in my day to day life.

Jesus saw the Will of the Father expressed in certain needs that invited Him to give an appropriate response. Likewise, each situation I am faced with carries in itself many needs. I cannot respond to every one of them. I must make a choice. Even then I may not be able to fulfill every possible demand of the need I have chosen. I must choose which response seems most appropriate in this specific situation in light of my unique self as illumined by the wisdom of Christ and His Church.

Different Christians, who sincerely follow Christ, will necessarily come to different responses. One Christian may enlist in the army to serve his country; another may become a conscientious objector. Both can be sincere followers of Christ. One follower of Christ may work within the established system for desirable social change; another may feel called to engage in less conventional methods. One follower may feel called to the spiritual enlightenment of the poor; another may do the same for the affluent. One follower may be a socializer; another may live a more hermitical life, imitating the hidden life of Christ. One may be more conservative, the other more progressive or middle of the road.

Demanded of the true follower is a prayerful immersion in the attitudes of Christ, a sincere self-appraisal on the vital, familial, cultural, spiritual, and actual levels of his life, and careful evaluation of his time and place. All of this must take place in light of the wisdom of the Church, which represents the living continuation of Christ among us.

Such immersion can instill in me certain lasting intuitions that will spontaneously shape my own words, actions, and attitudes in creative conformity to those of Jesus. I must learn to respond creatively and uniquely in ways that are congruent with the attitudes of Jesus yet conditioned by my own original personality and actual situation. The Christian life style can never be a facsimile imitation of a rigid outline of rules which would apply uniformly to all people in any given situation. Christianity is a life of divinely disciplined originality.

I will never be able to perfectly follow Jesus or to be perfectly faithful to my divine originality. Therefore life can only be bearable and joyous for me if I live it in the light of redemption. I may fail repeatedly but I know that my Redeemer lives.

## Three Ways of Following

We have mainly spoken thus far about my active following of Christ. I reflect on His life and in its light evaluate my situation. I try then to realize my task here and now, my profile of abilities and deficiencies in accordance with His life as it comes to me after my reflection on the Gospel.

This active way of following Jesus is not the only or, for that matter, the most perfect one. It is a first and necessary way of following. I may be restricted to this way for a lifetime. If this would be God's Will for me, I ought to accept it gladly. I may hope and pray, however, that He will lift me beyond this stage. For this active following of the Lord has many shortcomings.

It implies the somewhat cumbersome process of study, reflection, reasoning, experimentation, feeling, and imagining, and necessarily keeps me divided. I am scattered over all of these mental and emotional acts. I cannot yet be quietly at-one in my deepest self.

The active way of following also implies that I become aware of my originality. As long as I am a blind tentacle of the crowd or collectivity, no following of Christ is possible, for I do not know who I am. Even so, this necessary temporary preoccupation with self always carries with it a taint of egoism, a certain clinging to myself over against others. Active concern with my uniqueness makes it impossible for me to be wholly permeated by the awareness that I am nothing, that my uniqueness is given to me at every moment of my life, that I am an utterly dependent originality. The very nature of the active role I play in my original following of Jesus necessarily evokes a certain experience of self-sufficiency, a hidden feeling of independence.

To some degree I may purify myself of such feelings. They are so deeply rooted, however, in my fallen nature that I can never overcome them totally. The Lord Himself must take a hand in this. Otherwise union with Him in the deepest sense will not be possible for me in this life.

Another drawback of active following and the complexity of the mental operations implied in it, is the wide margin it leaves for error, self-deception, and illusion. My innate egoism may insert itself into the prolonged acts of reflection, reasoning, self-evaluation, and experimental imitation which occur during this process. The life and sayings of Jesus may become falsified; human self-interest is always there to spoil the divine message.

The same is true of my active attempts to know and live by my original calling. The more willful my attempt to hear and follow this call, the more my striving is in danger of being poisoned by egotistic needs, fears, and ambitions that parade as my real self.

The active following of Christ is thus a very imperfect way. Nevertheless, it is the only way open to me in the beginning. It would be a dangerous illusion to imagine that I am so far advanced in grace and wisdom that I could bypass this phase. Even to be restricted to this way for a lifetime—as many are—is infinitely better than no way. To try to discover my original self in the light of the life of Christ is far better than to be lost in the mass of men without a life of my own, even if active self-discovery will always be tainted by some degree of pride and self-deception. For without becoming a person, any form of spirituality will be impossible.

As we said earlier, I should hope and pray that the Lord will take me beyond this way. In that case, He will reverse the roles. I will no longer be following Christ by means of reflection and action alone, but Christ will make me follow Him by a mysterious urge and inspiration that wells up within me from His Presence in the deepest core of my being. I will experience Christ not only in the holy texts outside me but in my innermost self, where I originate continuously from Him the Eternal Word. I will become so at-one with Him that I do not know any longer who He is and who I am.

Only this event of deepest transformation in Christ can take away hidden pride in my originality and the constant falsification of this originality by my dominating ego. This mysterious point of my soul, where I originate uniquely from the Eternal Word, is far away from my surface consciousness. Grace may enable me to silently descend into that inner region that lies beyond conception, imagination, and discursive reasoning. There I will become aware that the ground and the substance of my originality is Christ Himself.

We could call this last way of following Christ—where He Himself takes over and I become receptive only—the way of identification. The active way we described earlier could then be divided in two ways, the way of "imitation" and the way of "intimacy." Grace plays a role in these two earlier ways too, only I am far more active than I will be in the way of identification.

### Imitation and Intimacy

When I am imitating Christ, I study carefully the pattern of His life. I compare it with my own life and situation. Then I try to adapt the pattern of His life to my situation. Imitation has its focus on the external pattern of the historical life of Jesus. It does not neglect His inner attitudes but attention is mainly focused on the words and behavior that reveal these attitudes as He lives them.

Gradually, the beginning follower of Christ becomes more aware of the inner feelings, mind, and attitudes of Jesus. My attention shifts, then, to the inner life of my Lord. I try to have in myself the same feelings and attitudes that were in Him. My following becomes more intimate and affective, less external and discursive. Soon I find myself in the phase of following what we called the way of intimacy. My discursive reasoning about His words and life becomes less dominant, but I am still active in my striving and feeling.

In imitation, I started out with an active transformation of my external behavior. I tried to be more Christ-like in my actions and appearance. This surely helped to purify me from behavior that was grossly at odds with the life of Christ. Because my acts do have an impact on my interiority, imitation prepared the way for my awareness of the intimate dimension of Christ's life and its meaning for me.

Now in this way of intimacy, I try to transform my original life in its inward emotional and attitudinal dimension. Reasoning decreases; my presence to Christ becomes more affective. Intellectual thought is complemented by felt aspiration. I aspire inwardly after the life of Christ. This aspiration may take the form of a simple prayer "My Lord and my God" or just the name of Jesus. I may repeat His words, feeling at-one with Him, for example, some words of the "Our Father," such as "Your will be done."

Because reasoning is less and less involved, my whole following becomes more simplified. Mine is not yet a total simplicity, however. My vital emotional self is much involved in this affective following of Jesus. Diversity and intensity of feeling may interrupt simple affective presence. Moreover, my feelings do have a history of self-centeredness. They do not necessarily represent the original me as it comes forth from the Eternal Word. My false self is still liable to taint my following. I cannot yet be my true original self in Christ. This means I cannot yet be truly Christ. Except for some extraordinary moments, I am still bound to experience my identity as totally separated from His.

I may be called like many to live in this way of intimacy for a life-time. This would already be a great grace to be accepted with gratitude. However, I should be ready to follow Christ in a deeper way, the way of receptivity and graced identification, if grace would invite me to it.

## Identification

In this way, I am not so much present to Christ as He becomes present to me in an undeniable mysterious manner. I feel bored with any attempt of reasoning, imagination, or vital emotion in my following of Him. I feel bored now with any preoccupation with my uniqueness and how it relates to living His life. On the positive side, there is, deep down, the delicate tender beginning of a spontaneous awareness of His Presence in my innermost self. This Presence is experienced as beyond any of my efforts, concepts, vital emotions, and imagination. He is somehow here in me. I am somehow in Him.

At such graced moments, I fail in any attempt to see Christ as my model separated from me, and to see myself as the eager imitator separated from Him. I entertain no longer clear and distinct ideas and images about the life of Jesus. Active imitation is out of the question. I want only to be wholly present to the silent Presence of Christ in me, to the welling up in me of His love for the Father. The time for silent at-oneness has come.

If I would tenaciously keep on trying to actively imitate Christ as a model offered to me for my study and observation, I would interfere with this beginning inner at-oneness with Christ. I should be quiet, receptive, still, wholly obedient and compliant with the new life that emerges in me. Otherwise I may smother the tiny awareness of the emergence of Jesus' life in my deepest self. Following Jesus means now to abandon myself to His emerging life in me.

I should not allow my managing me to struggle against the deeper me that is hidden in Him and that now begins to arise almost miraculously. I should remain receptively attentive to this silent wonder of new life, that is at the same time His and mine. The managing me must die as the dominant agent of my following of Christ. It must become only a tool, an instrument of the practical incarnation of the real me in Christ that now begins to reveal itself. Christ in me communicates to my whole life and being how He wants to live in my world in and through me.

Christ as the Eternal Word escapes all images, all models, postures, thoughts, descriptions, stories, and fantasies. He is the ineffable, the unspeakable, the inexpressible. He is the wordless mystery at the beginning of all people; events, and things. He is the innermost originality of their originality. He was before everything existed. He is the pristine form, the inner model of any creature. He holds all things in oneness, while infinitely respecting their diversity and uniqueness.

The deepest thing in me is not me but Christ. It is not I who live but Christ who lives in me. He is the original me before I was born. Christ is deep down in me as my true self; He is in me not as a model of imitation but as my inmost inspiration.

In this receptive way of the following of Christ, I no longer ask myself, as I did in the active way, "What would Christ do in this situation?" or "How would He take into account my original calling and personal history?" My response to the situation emerges spontaneously, undeniably from my deepest self. There I am aware of Christ and His answer beyond questions, concepts, and images. Words, concepts, and images of Christ are not Christ. He can be known without ideas. He can be known in the spiritual poverty and darkness of faith.

The Scriptures point to Christ. But I may become so occupied with these splendid pointers that I miss the person to whom they are pointing. I should comply when the Lord gently urges me to go beyond Him as a model in order to find Him as life of my life, originality of my originality, aspiration of my aspiration. Here Jesus and my deepest originality are at-one.

To be sure, the Eternal Word at the core of my being is not divorced from the historical Christ of the Gospels whom I meditated on, especially when I travelled the ways of imitation and intimacy. There is no discontinuity between the Jesus of Israel and the Jesus in me who originates me in my originality. It is precisely in and through the Jesus of the Gospels and the Church that I come home to the Christ who is the most original me. For this reason the way of imitation is necessary. Moreover, no matter how deeply He draws me into the way of passive identification, I must return periodically to the historical humanity of Jesus.

In this final stage of following, I do not, so to speak, follow Jesus. Jesus makes me follow Him in my most original way—a way He knows infinitely better than I do because it is hidden in Him from eternity.

I am no longer active in the sense of actively managing. My activity is a passive following of or flowing with the activity of Jesus in me. My presence to Him is immensely simplified. So too is my active willing and striving. The managing me is held in the poverty of not managing, not knowing, not striving. Without any solicitude whatsoever for my self, I am present in and through and with Jesus to the Divine and His mysterious Will in which all creation is immersed. My whole original life, all my deeds, feelings, willing, and planning begin to grow from that Presence.

Christ, the Eternal Word, is the first and foremost originality of all creatures. After my clumsy active attempts to purify my originality, I allow Him to purify

it and to restore it to what it was meant to be from
eternity. This purification by Christ is a sharing in His
detachment, passion, and death. My death is the
anguished loss of a false self so that my true self may
arise and be divinized. Christ in me is the divinization of
my original self that was from eternity in Him.

> Through Him,
> with Him,
> in Him,
> in the unity of the Holy Spirit
> all glory and honor is Yours
> almighty Father
> for ever and ever.

ODaU-M